Copyright © 2022
Best Friends Animal Society

ISBN 9798363964633

The information in this book is provided for entertainment and/or informational purposes only and should be used at your own discretion. As with any food you prepare for yourself, your family or others (including your pets), you should do your own research and consult with your health care providers and anyone who will be consuming the food you prepare to determine whether the ingredients and recipes in this book are appropriate for your and their consumption. Best Friends Animal Society makes no warranty relating to the accuracy, completeness, or results of any of the information, or your use of the information, contained in this book. Accordingly, any use of the recipes, ingredients or any other information in this book will be at your sole discretion, that you assume full responsibility for doing so, and Best Friends Animal Society will not be responsible for any resulting loss or damages, of any type, whether direct or indirect.

The Best Friends Cookbook

Where kindness fills the kitchen

Best Friends

This book is dedicated to all those who have been to Best Friends Animal Sanctuary and joined us for lunch. For those yet to visit this special place, we hope you join us one day.

We also dedicate this book to Best Friends co-founder Faith Maloney. A lifelong vegan, Faith had lunch at the Angel Village café every day for years. Each day she shared her table and conversation with visitors. Faith passed away in 2022. Lunch won't be the same without her. But what she taught us all about hospitality lives on.

We are so pleased to share these recipes from the inspired cooks at Angel Village café. To all who support Best Friends, we are grateful.

Faith Maloney, Best Friends co-founder, and Shade.

Table of Contents

Introduction: Welcome to the kindness kitchen 9

Angel Village café: More than just a cafeteria 11

The history of Angel Village café 13

PREP YOUR PANTRY

Prep your pantry 18

BREAKFAST

Rise and Sunshine Scramble 22

Peaches and Cream Pancakes 25

French Toast 26

Do-it-yourself Muesli 27

Cherry Almond Mini-Scones 28

SALADS

Spicy Lemon Pepper Pasta Salad 34

Chickpea Salad 36

Parrot Chop for People 38

Street Corn Salad 40

MAIN MEALS

Garden Couscous 46

'Cheeseburger' Penne 48

White Bean Stew 49

Moussaka 50

Thai Tempeh in Peanut Sauce 53

Pasta with Sausage and Kale 54

BBQ Jackfruit 56

Tamale Pie 57

Korean Street Tacos 58

Cashew Lettuce Wraps 61
Super Sloppy Joes 63
Bark Mi: Best Friends Bánh Mì 64
Mushroom Stroganoff 66
Chimichurri Enchiladas 68
'Tuna' Casserole 70
Pineapple Fried Rice 72

APPETIZERS, SIDES & SAUCES
Southwest Medley 78
Tomato and Avocado 'Caprese' Toast 80
Mediterranean Mezze Platter 83
Baba Ghanoush 84
Hummus 85
Tzatziki 85
Stovetop Baked Beans 86
Cashews Two Ways, Sweet and Savory 87

DESSERTS
Lemon Pie Chia Pudding 93
Pumpkin Chocolate Chip Cookies 94
Peanut Butter Cookies 96
PB&C Avocado Mousse with Vanilla Cashew Cream 97
Mini-Churro Twists 98

RECIPES FOR YOUR PET
Barkcuterie Board 105
Parrot Chop for Parrots 106
Parrot Pops 106
Kitty Upside-down Cake 108

Best Friends Animal Sanctuary: There's no place like home. 111
Acknowledgments 112

Introduction

Welcome to the kindness kitchen!

Here at Best Friends, kindness to animals extends to the kitchen. Come cook with us!

At the Best Friends Animal Sanctuary, we have fed many a hard-working animal lover. Our Angel Village café serves fresh plant-based foods to nourish peoples' bodies and show kindness to the planet. Fact: Plant foods use far fewer resources than animal foods, they honor local agricultural traditions and they taste so darn delicious!

Since 1984, Best Friends Animal Society has worked to change the face of animal welfare by creating a better world through kindness to animals. Our devotion to kindness means we know a thing or two about scrumptious, plant-based dining. This book shares with you some of our favorite stories and recipes. Please enjoy these homey, yummy dishes for entertaining friends or just curling up solo to feed your soul. There is real comfort in cooking with plants.

We are so glad you found this cookbook. Rest assured, all of the recipes are dairy-free. If you also can't eat gluten, simply use gluten-free flour, pasta and breads as called for in the recipes.

Lunch has never been loftier! Try the cashew lettuce wraps, the street corn salad, the mushroom stroganoff or indulge yourself at the epic salad bar. We guarantee the desserts will make your taste buds smile. Plant-based food has never tasted so good. Thanks to the inspired Angel Village café menu, the stunning views and the patio tables perched on the mesa, we created this cookbook. We hope it gives you wings.

Angel Village café: More than just a cafeteria

You can get a delicious, vegan meal for only $5, but most people walk away from Angel Village café with more than a full belly. The café is somewhere for like-minded people to come, chat, share stories, gain a sense of community and refuel after a morning of caring for the animals.

The founders of Best Friends are regular guests here. When they were first building Best Friends Animal Sanctuary, they would come here to relax and take in the beautiful canyon view after long, hard days. The kitchen we use was their community kitchen and the offices down the hall were their bedrooms. One of the founders always jokes that "The view is $5 and the food is free!" Each day, Angel Village café feeds 150-200 staff members. My team and I take pride in fostering a welcoming and friendly atmosphere. We try to create meals for everyone to enjoy — meals that are also kind to animals and the environment. I love working in the café for many reasons: the view, the staff, the guests, the food. The list goes on. I hope this book will bring some of those feelings we have in the café right into your home.

BriAnne Figgins

Manager, Angel Village café with Maze and Max

"There were just a few of us 'crazy ones' who thought we could change the world by saving homeless pets. We were the founders of Best Friends. We arrived in Kanab, Utah, in 1984 and started building what would become Best Friends Animal Sanctuary, five miles north of town in Angel Canyon."

– Cyrus Mejia, co-founder

The history of Angel Village café

We all had to learn new skills. Since I was an artist, I learned to handle a sprayer and painted lots of walls. One day, Faith Maloney, another Best Friends founder, noticed how carefully I was preparing my breakfast. She said, "Hey, it looks like you're good at cooking. Why don't you make lunch for everyone?" So, I became the cook, and that was the beginning of Angel Village café.

I had just become a vegan back then, so my meals were all plant-based: no meat, no dairy, no eggs. There are three very important reasons for eating a totally plant-based diet. It's good for the animals. It's good for the earth. It's good for your health.

When I first started cooking in the village café, I didn't need a lot of recipes. It was just Best Friends staff and the occasional visitor sharing the meals. But I didn't want to serve the same thing every meal, so research and development was a big part of my job — which was fine until my dogs got involved. How do you tell a 100-pound black Lab that you don't need his critique of every single recipe?

One day, the local grocery store owner pulled me aside and surprised me with a question. In those days, plant-based cooking was not exactly mainstream. In fact, it was pretty far out there. But he said more and more folks were being told by their doctors to eat less meat, and they were asking him about plant-based products like tofu and tempeh, which he was ordering for us. He couldn't answer all their questions, so he asked if I would teach a cooking class in the deli kitchen. Of course, I said yes, and with promotion from the grocery store, we soon had a regular group of local folks learning about vegan cooking. That's how great things get started, one meal and one class and one sanctuary at a time.

The village café now serves hundreds of delicious, plant-based lunches for staff, volunteers and visitors. And what started out as a small group of "nuts" rescuing animals in the desert has grown to become a national organization, leading the movement to stop the killing of pets in shelters. I am overflowing with gratitude to you, our members and supporters. So many compassionate people have contributed over the years to make this dream become an incredible reality. Thank you.

Cyrus Mejia
Co-founder, board member, Best Friends Animal Society with Roxy

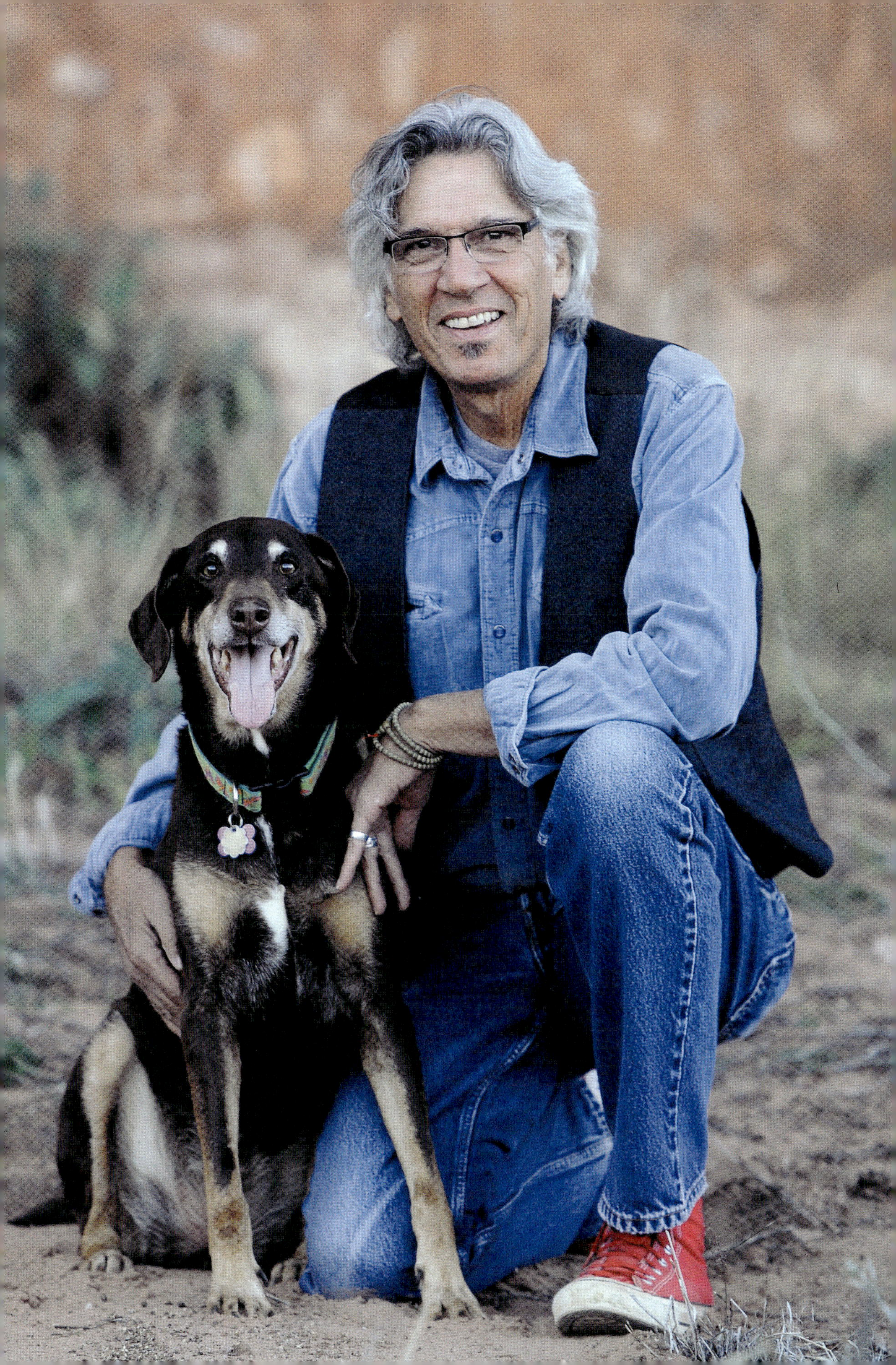

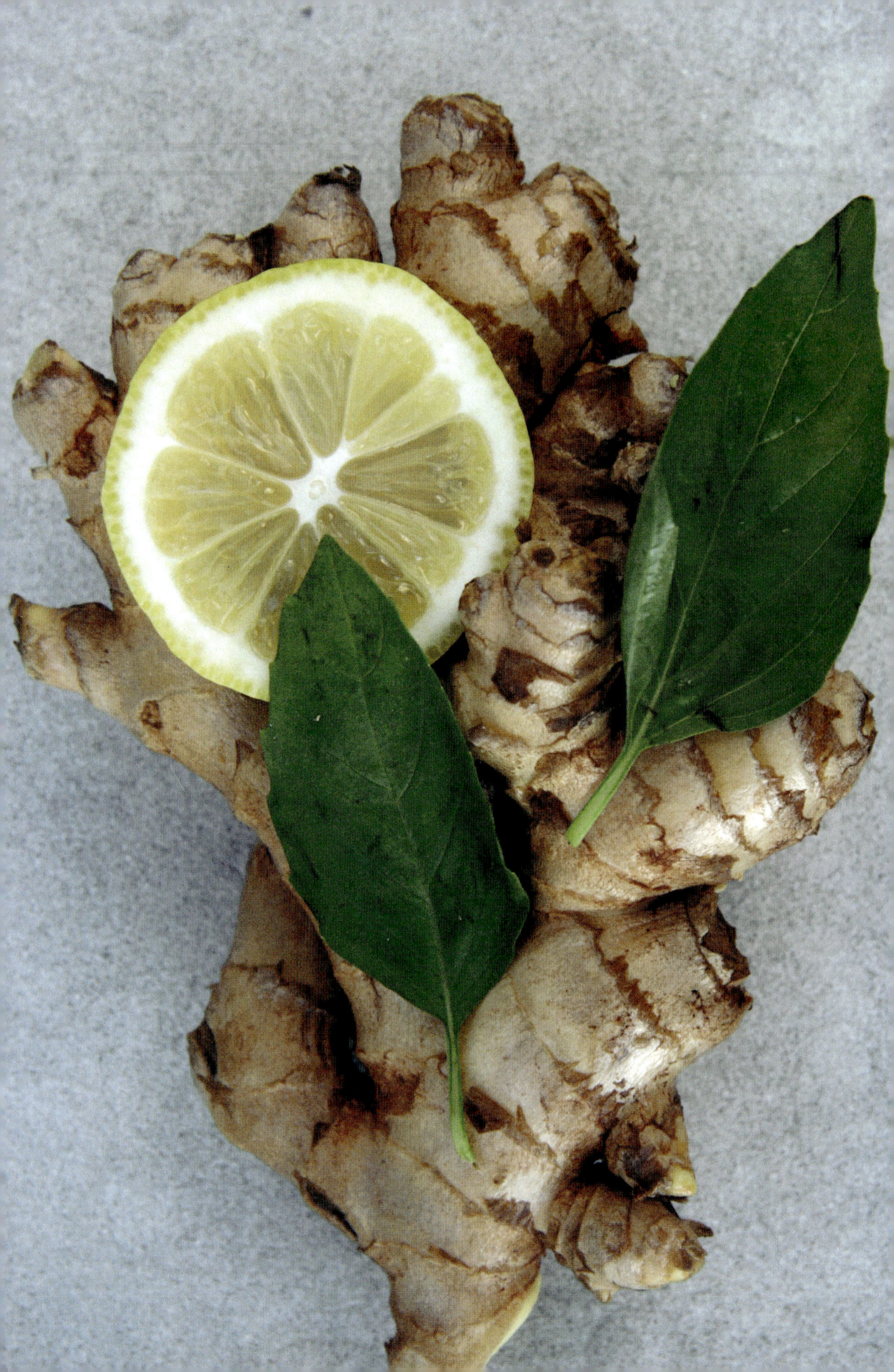

Prep Your Pantry

Prep your pantry

You don't have to revolutionize your kitchen to enjoy wholesome, homemade food. But you should have a few ingredients on hand to help you create deliciousness. Cooking is so much easier when you don't have to dash out to the store before every meal.

Cooking with plant-based foods is all about inspiration and savvy food substitutions. Here are a few of the tried-and-true ingredients called for in the Best Friends Cookbook. You don't have to buy the whole list right away. Just shop for ingredients each time you try a new recipe. Then, when you love the results, those ingredients will become staples on your grocery list. Of course, you'll need lots of fresh fruits and vegetables, too. That's an added pleasure of plant-based cooking: communing with produce. Better still, head out to a farmer's market or a local produce stand for the freshest, in-season options. Have fun exploring your options and stocking your pantry!

Beans
Pinto beans, chickpeas (also known as garbanzo beans) and cannellini beans are just a few of our favorites. They are high in fiber and protein, packed with nutrients, play well with spices and they're so easy to incorporate into recipes. Opt for "low sodium" or "no salt added."

Cacao powder
Who doesn't love chocolate? Cacao powder keeps all the chocolate taste and cuts the high fat content of cocoa butter. You get rich chocolate pleasure, and your heart says thanks.

Cashews
Raw cashews are your best sauce friend. When blended with a few other ingredients, raw cashews will satisfy your craving for rich, cheesy dips.

Chia seeds
Chia seeds are packed with omega-3 fatty acids and calcium. They make great pudding and amp up smoothies. When toasted, they quickly add crunch to anything.

Chickpeas
Also known as garbanzo beans, chickpeas make the best sandwich spread we've ever tried (no kidding). And they are the star players in hummus. If you buy one ingredient now, we suggest canned chickpeas.

Coarse sugar
Choose a minimally processed natural sugar like turbinado. Our recipes don't use lots of sugar but when they do, turbinado is a great ingredient to have on hand.

Coconut milk
This is a rich-flavored, thick milk used in cooking. We opt for light, canned coconut milk because it has less fat than full fat coconut milk but plenty of taste.

Dijon mustard
Let the French help you make irresistible meals. Dijon mustard adds bite and complexity to any recipe it touches. Plus, it's wonderful on appetizers, too.

Egg-free mayo
There are delicious egg-free varieties of mayonnaise at your grocery store. Try a few and pick a favorite.

Flax meal
Flax meal has a nutty flavor and many health benefits. It is an excellent binder when combined with water. Want to make an egg without a chicken? Try whipping up a "flax meal egg." It also works well in baked goods.

Fresh garlic heads
Nothing packs a taste punch like fresh garlic. Raw, sautéed, blended, roasted: Garlic cloves make magic. Crush the cloves before dicing them for maximum flavor.

Maple syrup
You'll be surprised just how deeply maple syrup improves flavors. It is a high-calorie food but you only use a little in our recipes. Plus, it is nature's own sugar gift.

Nondairy milk
There are so many choices of nondairy milk — rice, soy and almond, to name three. Choose the flavor and texture you prefer. They all work well in our recipes.

Nondairy butter
We don't use lots of butter but a hint of butter flavor can really make the difference. And if you are jonesing for a bowl of hot popcorn, you're going to need a "butter" drizzle.

Nutritional yeast
Yeast sounds boring but this ingredient has a cheesy flavor that elevates sauces and creams. Yeast is a member of the fungus kingdom that we don't want to do without.

Olive oil
A good olive oil makes all the difference. By good, we mean fresh-pressed and extra-virgin. Always choose a dark glass bottle or tin. Light quickly drains flavor away from olive oil.

Pasta
Don't stop at spaghetti noodles. Buy penne, rotini, bowties and ziti. Every shape of pasta has its own visual punch and different powers of sauce retention. And there are gluten-free versions of all shapes of pasta, too.

Quinoa
Quinoa comes from the beautiful flowering amaranth plant whose seeds are rich in protein, vitamins and minerals. It is quicker to cook than rice and readily absorbs flavors.

Rolled oats
Yes, you can cook with any kind of oats but we prefer rolled oats. They are an old-fashioned favorite, minimally processed and, when cooked, chewy and nutty.

Toasted sesame oil
A dash of sesame oil makes a meal distinctive. For more than three thousand years, humans have been growing and crushing sesame seeds for their oil.

Soy sauce
Some cooks like low-sodium soy sauce. Some cooks prefer tamari for a nonwheat option. Whatever sauce you choose, expect a bright taste of salt and the mysterious, savory flavor of umami.

Spices
A beautiful entry into the world of flavor, spices make all the difference and give a burst of flavor with healthful benefits. For heat, keep on hand some cayenne, curry powder, chili powder and red pepper flakes. Turmeric, cumin and coriander add depth. Garlic powder is a great fix when you're out of fresh garlic. Paprika comes in two types, hot and sweet. Use sweet if you're just garnishing the top of a casserole. Of course, we love fresh basil, oregano, thyme and dill, but you'll want to have dried versions on hand, too. And cinnamon, allspice and nutmeg are key ingredients for desserts.

Tahini
Hello again, sesame seeds. Tahini is made from crushed sesame seeds. It's like peanut butter, only made with seeds instead of nuts. Tahini has a subtly bitter taste that blends well with lemon and garlic. It's the key flavor that makes hummus shine.

Tempeh
Tofu, move over. You have a partner in plant-based proteins. Tempeh is made from fermented soybeans. It tastes nutty with hints of mushroom. If you are allergic to soy, it's best to steer clear of both tempeh and tofu.

Tofu
Buy blocks of organic tofu in whatever consistency you like: soft, silken, firm or extra-firm. Tofu makes great breakfast scrambles and loves to soak up the flavors of a marinade.

Vegetable broth
For soups, stews and sauces, you'll want to keep broth on hand. You can make your own vegetable broth, buy it in a carton or use the delicious veggie bouillon that comes in a jar. Bouillon costs less than packaged broth and tastes great.

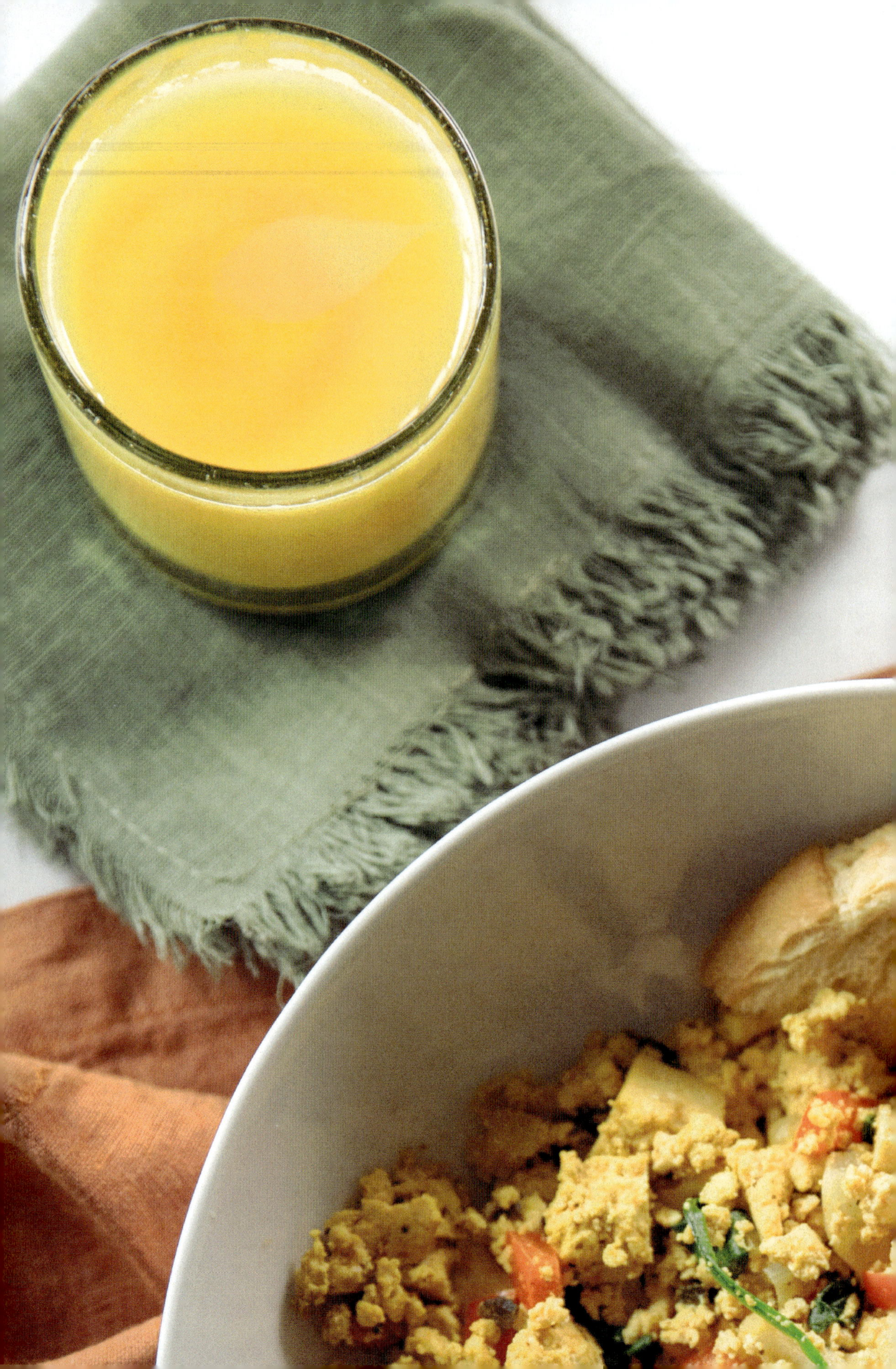

Breakfast

Rise and Sunshine Scramble

Serves 4

Ingredients

1 tablespoon oil

1 cup diced onion

1 cup diced bell pepper (any color)

1 cup diced mushrooms (button, cremini or other mushrooms of choice)

1 14-ounce block firm or extra firm tofu, drained

¾ teaspoon salt (or use kala namak for an eggy flavor)

¼ teaspoon black pepper

2 tablespoons nutritional yeast

½ teaspoon paprika

¼ teaspoon turmeric

1 teaspoon garlic powder

1 teaspoon Dijon mustard

1 cup chopped spinach

Squeeze of lemon

For a Mediterranean scramble, add:

1 teaspoon dried oregano

¼ cup chopped Kalamata olives

½ cup chopped tomatoes

1 tablespoon of lemon juice

For a Southwest scramble, add:

1 teaspoon chili powder

½ teaspoon cumin

1 can black beans, drained and rinsed

½ cup chopped tomatoes

Top with salsa of choice

For a curry scramble, add:

1 to 2 tablespoons curry powder

½ cup peas

Directions

Heat a large stovetop pan over medium-high heat. Add the oil, followed by the onions, bell peppers and mushrooms, cooking until the onions are soft and translucent, about 5-7 minutes. Crumble the tofu into the pan and cook, stirring often, for about 8 minutes or until most of the water from the tofu has evaporated. (This will depend on how much moisture your tofu contains.) Add the seasonings and stir to incorporate. Cook another 2-3 minutes. Fold in the spinach until it's tender. Serve with toast or as a side dish in a larger breakfast spread.

Notes

BREAKFAST

Feeling creative? Add extra veggies. (Just keep in mind, you may need to adjust your spices.) Toss in some chopped zucchini or even a can of beans for an extra protein boost. After cooking, top with fresh arugula, microgreens or sprouts for added greens and a pop of flavor!

Feeling creative? Add a dash of cinnamon or cacao powder to make a variety of flavors. Use vanilla nondairy yogurt in place of the cashew cream.

Peaches and Cream Pancakes

Serves 2

Ingredients

1 medium banana

1 cup rolled oats

½ cup nondairy milk

1 tablespoon maple syrup

1 teaspoon baking powder

1 tablespoon apple cider vinegar

1 teaspoon vanilla extract

1 pinch salt

½ cup peaches, fresh, frozen, or canned and drained

½ cup chopped pecans (or pumpkin seeds for nut-free)

Vanilla cashew cream (optional, see page 87)

Directions

Add the first eight ingredients to a food processor or blender and blend for 2–3 minutes until smooth.

Transfer to a medium bowl and stir in the peaches and pecans (or seeds).

Depending on your griddle, you may need a bit of vegetable oil to prevent pancakes from sticking. Spoon the pancake mixture onto the griddle with a ladle to form four-inch round pancakes, which will give you approximately eight in total. Cook on each side until golden brown, and top with vanilla cashew cream or maple syrup.

Notes

_____

_____

_____

_____

_____

_____

BREAKFAST

French Toast

Makes 4 to 6 pieces of toast

Ingredients

2 tablespoons flour

2 tablespoons nutritional yeast

½ teaspoon salt

1 teaspoon sugar

½ teaspoon ground cinnamon

1 cup nondairy milk of choice

1 tablespoon tahini

2 tablespoons oil

4 to 6 slices bread (ideally, firmer bread)

Nondairy butter, to taste

Maple syrup, to taste

Directions

Mix dry ingredients together in a medium or large bowl, then whisk in the milk, tahini and oil to make a batter.

Heat a skillet over medium heat and lightly spray with oil. Dip bread into the batter, coating both sides, and fry until lightly browned and crispy on both sides (about 5 minutes).

Serve with nondairy butter and maple syrup.

Feeling creative? For more nutrition, use whole grain or sprouted whole grain bread. Top with fresh fruit of choice. Add some nondairy sour cream or nondairy yogurt of choice. Top with your favorite nuts or seeds.

Notes

Do-it-yourself Muesli

Serves 1 (easily multiplied for additional servings)

Ingredients

½ cup rolled oats

1 tablespoon raisins or other dried fruit

¼ cup fresh or frozen blueberries or other fresh fruit (such as strawberries or bananas)

¼ cup chopped nuts and/or seeds of choice, in any combination (such as walnuts, pecans, hazelnuts, pumpkin seeds, sunflower seeds, etc.)

½-1 cup nondairy milk

1 teaspoon maple syrup, optional

Pinch of salt

Directions

Add the oats, raisins, blueberries and nuts or seeds to a cereal bowl. Pour nondairy milk, maple syrup (if using) and a pinch of salt on top. Stir to combine.

Feeling creative? Toast your oats in a dry pan for a nutty flavor, or presoak them in a few tablespoons of water with a bit of lemon juice before mixing for added zest.

BREAKFAST

Cherry Almond Mini-Scones

Makes about 16 scones

Ingredients

1 tablespoon flax meal (can substitute with 1 tablespoon of egg replacer mixed with water according to package instructions)

3 tablespoons water

1⅓ cups flour

2 tablespoons sugar

½ teaspoon salt

1½ teaspoons baking powder

¼ cup nondairy butter, cold

1 teaspoon vanilla extract

¼ cup nondairy milk, plus 1 tablespoon extra for brushing

½ cup chopped fresh or frozen (thawed and drained) sweet cherries

¼ cup slivered almonds, optional

1 tablespoon coarse sugar, such as turbinado cane sugar

Directions

Preheat oven to 350 degrees F. Make your flax egg by mixing the flax and water in a small bowl and set aside. In a large bowl add flour, sugar, salt, baking powder and mix well. Cube cold butter and cut it into the flour mixture until pea-size dough balls are formed. Add cherries and almonds (if using) and toss until coated in flour. Add the flax egg, vanilla and milk, and stir until just combined. Gently fold the dough until it all sticks together (about 15 seconds). Using a cookie scoop or spoon, scoop golf ball-size scones onto a baking sheet, about 2 inches apart, and bake for 13-16 minutes or until golden. Once out of the oven, brush the tops with nondairy milk and sprinkle with coarse sugar.

Notes _____

_____

_____

_____

BREAKFAST

Feeling creative? To make the scones more nutritious, use oat flour or whole wheat flour, and use coconut sugar in place of granulated sugar. For nut-free, omit the almonds or use sunflower or pumpkin seeds. For extra almond flavor, use almond extract in place of vanilla extract. Use blueberries, chopped strawberries or even chocolate chips instead of cherries.

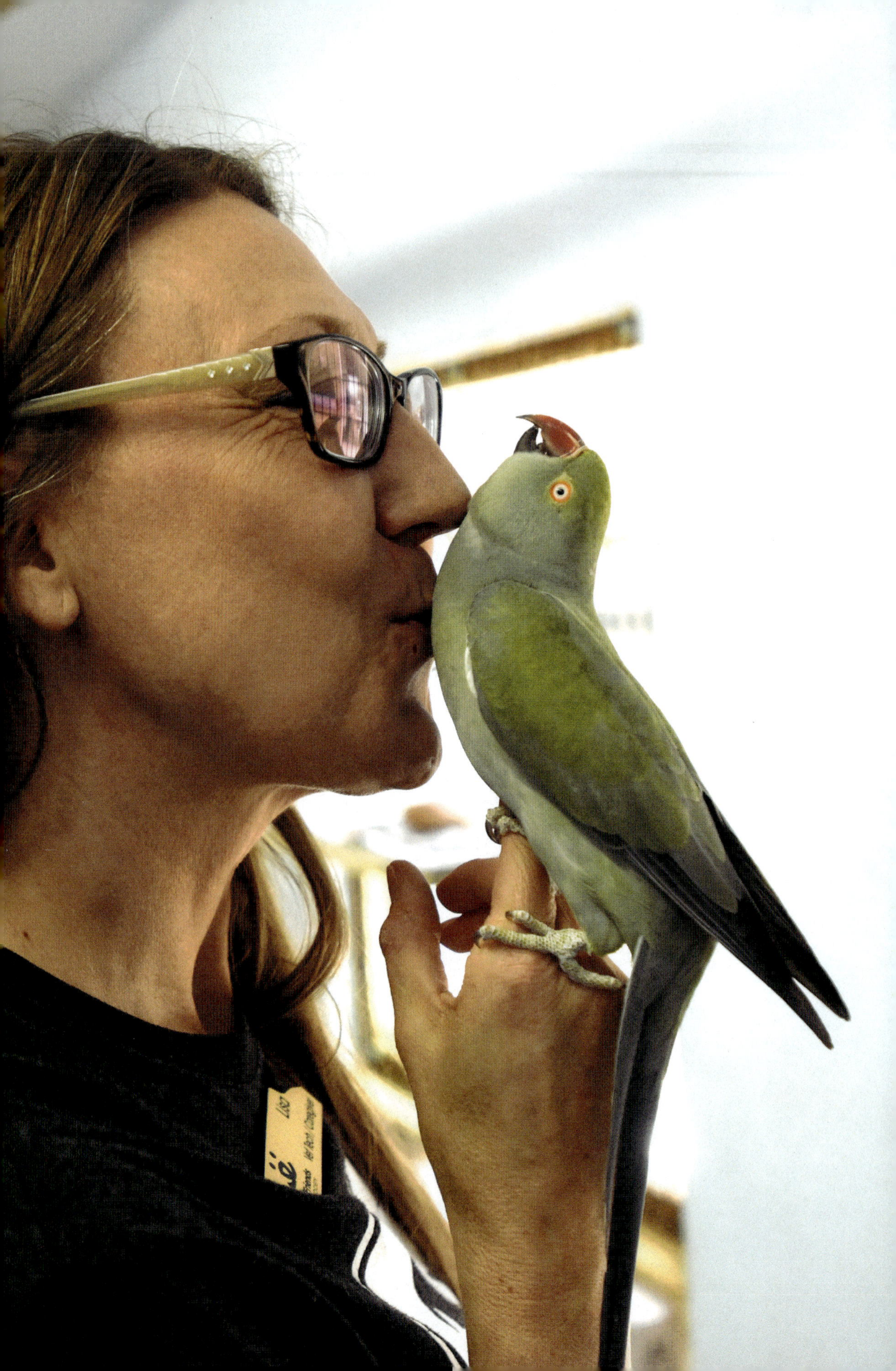

This good big change

I grew up in northern Minnesota where we commonly ate meat, some form of potatoes and, as a Scandinavian, the occasional lutefisk. Since I loved animals passionately, I gravitated toward eating grains, vegetables and fruits. Fast forward to April Fool's Day 2002, when I declared to my family that I was going vegetarian. They thought that I was kidding but 20 years later, this good big change is still no joke.

I love to cook and explore delicious flavors, so I gave myself a gift subscription to a vegetarian magazine. One day, while going through the latest issue, I saw an article highlighting five nonprofits worthy of checking out. One of them was Best Friends Animal Society and it included a photo of horses running at full gallop in a meadow, manes and tails blowing in the wind, surrounded by red rocks in a place referenced as Angel Canyon. The first thought I had: This beautiful place just simply cannot exist. I mean, c'mon. Is this even real?

Soon after, I visited the Sanctuary to see for myself if it was as magical as that photo said. I quickly discovered that it was not — because it was even more magical, beautiful, kind, generous and loving than any photo could ever capture. Angel Canyon holds a special magic. It's a connection to the past. It reminds us of our responsibilities. It's inspirational.

I did return to Minnesota but only to be sure that my heart had found its new home in Utah. I decided then and there to move to Kanab to work for Best Friends.

It all began with one choice, one decision. And now, how lucky am I? Because of a vegetarian magazine article about Best Friends, I get to support animal welfare in many ways: through the food I eat, the cruelty-free products I use, the materials I choose to wear and, as luck would have it, in my daily work and livelihood at Best Friends. I'm hoping that by hearing my story and enjoying the recipes in this cookbook, perhaps your life might change, too.

Lisa
Best Friends employee with Gray Dancer

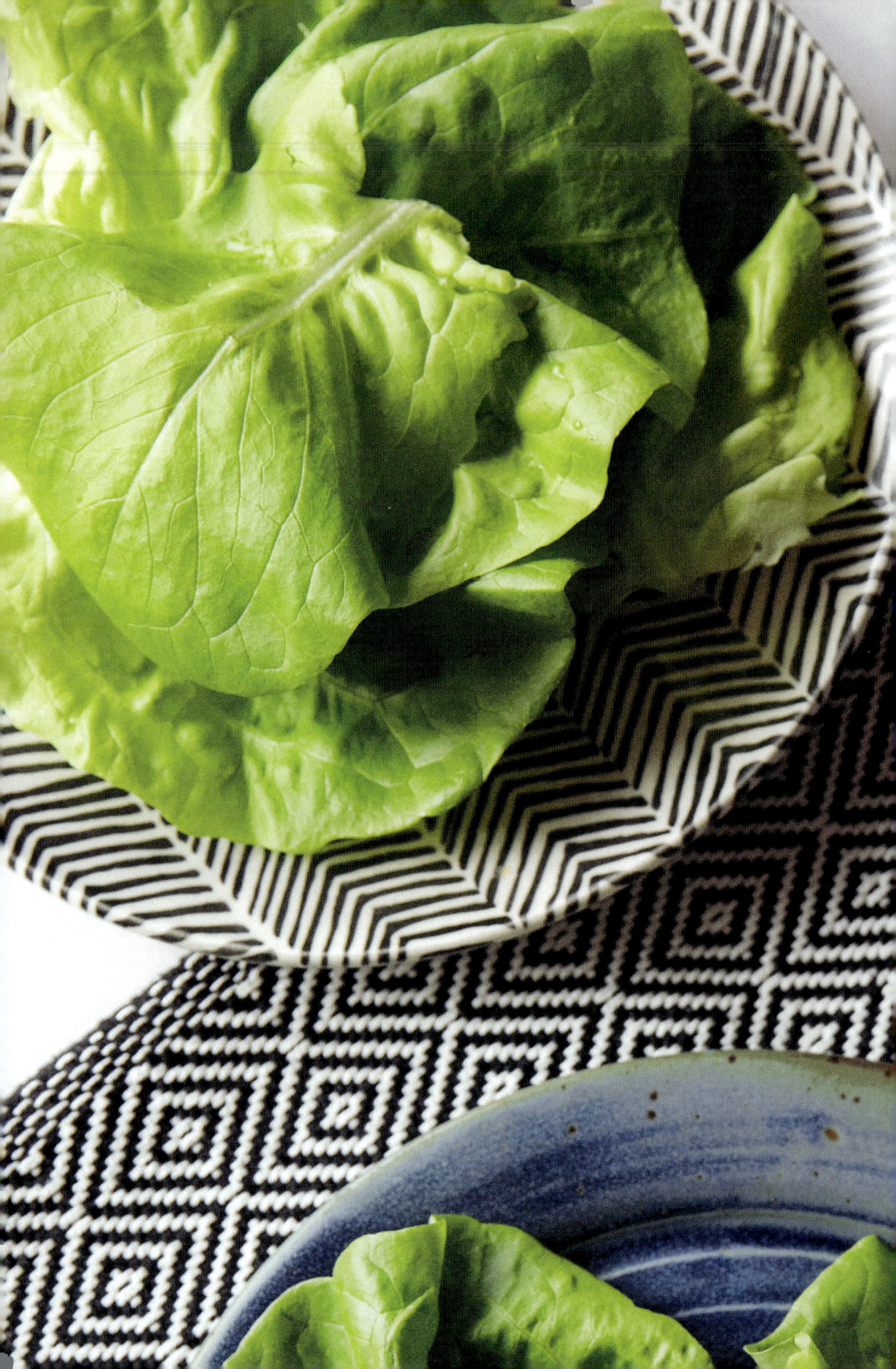

Salads

Spicy Lemon Pepper Pasta Salad

Serves 4

Ingredients

8 ounces bow tie pasta or other pasta of choice

2 tablespoons oil

1 tablespoon lemon juice

½ teaspoon red pepper flakes (optional)

½ teaspoon salt, plus more to taste, if desired

¼ teaspoon black pepper, plus more to taste

2 cups chopped raw broccoli

½ cup chopped sun-dried tomatoes

Lemon zest, optional for garnish and flavor

Directions

Cook pasta according to package directions, drain and rinse with cold water. Set aside.

In a large bowl, whisk together the oil, lemon juice, red pepper flakes, salt and pepper.

Add the broccoli, sun-dried tomatoes and cooked pasta to the bowl with the dressing and stir to combine ingredients. Add more salt and pepper to taste.

Top with lemon zest (if using) and serve.

Notes

Feeling creative? To make it more nutritious, use legume or whole-grain pasta, add more veggies such as chopped spinach, fresh tomatoes or mushrooms, and top with chopped basil and nutritional yeast. Add a cup of beans, peas or lentils to add protein.

Chickpea Salad

Serves 4

Ingredients

15-ounce can of chickpeas, drained and rinsed (or 1½ cups homemade chickpeas)

½ cup shredded carrots

1 stalk celery, diced

¼ cup diced red onion

½ cup egg-free mayo

2 tablespoons minced fresh dill

1 teaspoon onion powder

½ teaspoon salt

½ teaspoon pepper

Directions

Add the chickpeas to a large bowl and smash with a potato masher or the back of a fork. You want to mash them quite a bit but still leave some chunks intact.

Add the carrots, celery, onion, mayo, dill, onion powder, salt and pepper. Mix well and taste, adjusting seasoning if necessary.

Serve in a sandwich with pita bread, eat with crackers or enjoy the salad on its own.

Notes

Feeling creative? For a "chicken" salad, use 10 ounces of diced, cooked meatless chicken instead of chickpeas and replace carrots with ½ cup halved grapes or ¼ cup dried cranberries. Make it more nutritious by scooping the salad into lettuce wraps, or use other greens like collards or Swiss chard for the wrap.

Parrot Chop for People

Serves 4

Ingredients

1 cup dry quinoa (or about 3 cups cooked)

2 cups shredded purple cabbage

2 cups chopped snap peas

1 cup shredded carrot

1 cup diced red bell pepper

1 cup diced fresh mango

1½ cups beans of choice (such as edamame, black beans or chickpeas)

½ cup nuts of choice (such as chopped peanuts, slivered almonds or sunflower seeds for nut-free)

Chili powder, for garnish

Salt and pepper to taste

Dressing

½ cup canned coconut milk

½ cup unsweetened peanut or almond butter

¼ cup soy sauce or reduced sodium tamari

¼ cup orange juice

Juice of 1 lime

Pinch of cayenne (optional)

Directions

Cook the quinoa according to package instructions, then set aside to cool while you prepare everything else. Add all the veggies and beans to a bowl along with the cooked and cooled quinoa and combine. Whisk together the dressing ingredients in a separate bowl, then pour into the veggie/quinoa mixture. Mix everything together and top with nuts of your choice. Add salt and pepper to taste. For garnish and a little flavor, sprinkle chili powder on top, if desired.

Notes

SALADS

Feeling creative? Use cubed, baked tofu in place of the beans. Substitute millet, couscous or other grain in place of quinoa. Use pineapple or mandarin oranges instead of mango for variety. Try chopped broccoli in place of the peas or shredded beets in place of the carrots. Use whatever vegetables you have that are colorful and fresh.

Street Corn Salad

Serves 6 as a side dish

Ingredients

⅓ cup egg-free mayo

1 lime, zested and juiced

Pinch of cayenne or more to taste (optional)

1 teaspoon salt

½ teaspoon pepper

1 tablespoon oil

16-ounce bag frozen corn, thawed

1 cup diced red onion

1 tablespoon minced garlic

1 pint cherry tomatoes, halved

6 to 8 radishes, thinly sliced (about half a cup)

½ cup fresh chopped cilantro

¼ cup DIY Parmesan (optional)

DIY Parmesan

Using a high-speed blender (such as a Vitamix or Blendtec), blend 1 cup of your favorite toasted nuts or seeds (walnuts and sunflower seeds work well) with 1 to 2 tablespoons of nutritional yeast, plus salt, to taste, until the mixture reaches a soft, crumbly consistency. Don't over-blend or else you'll have walnut Parmesan butter!

Directions

In a large bowl, mix the egg-free mayo, lime zest and juice, cayenne (if using), salt and pepper, and set aside the dressing.

In a large skillet, heat the oil over medium-high heat and add in the onion. Cook for about 3-4 minutes, stirring occasionally, then add in the corn. Stir to combine it with the onions but then let the corn and onions cook without stirring. Resist the temptation to stir! That way, the corn gets nice and charred. Stir once more, and then let the onions and corn cook again for a few more minutes. When the corn is charred and the onions are soft, stir in the garlic and cook for another 30 seconds. Remove from heat.

Toss the tomatoes, radishes and corn mixture into the bowl with the dressing and stir to combine. Top with cilantro and nondairy Parmesan (if using).

Notes

SALADS

Feeling creative? Substitute other veggies of your choice for the radish, such as jicama or red cabbage. Substitute parsley or chives for the cilantro.

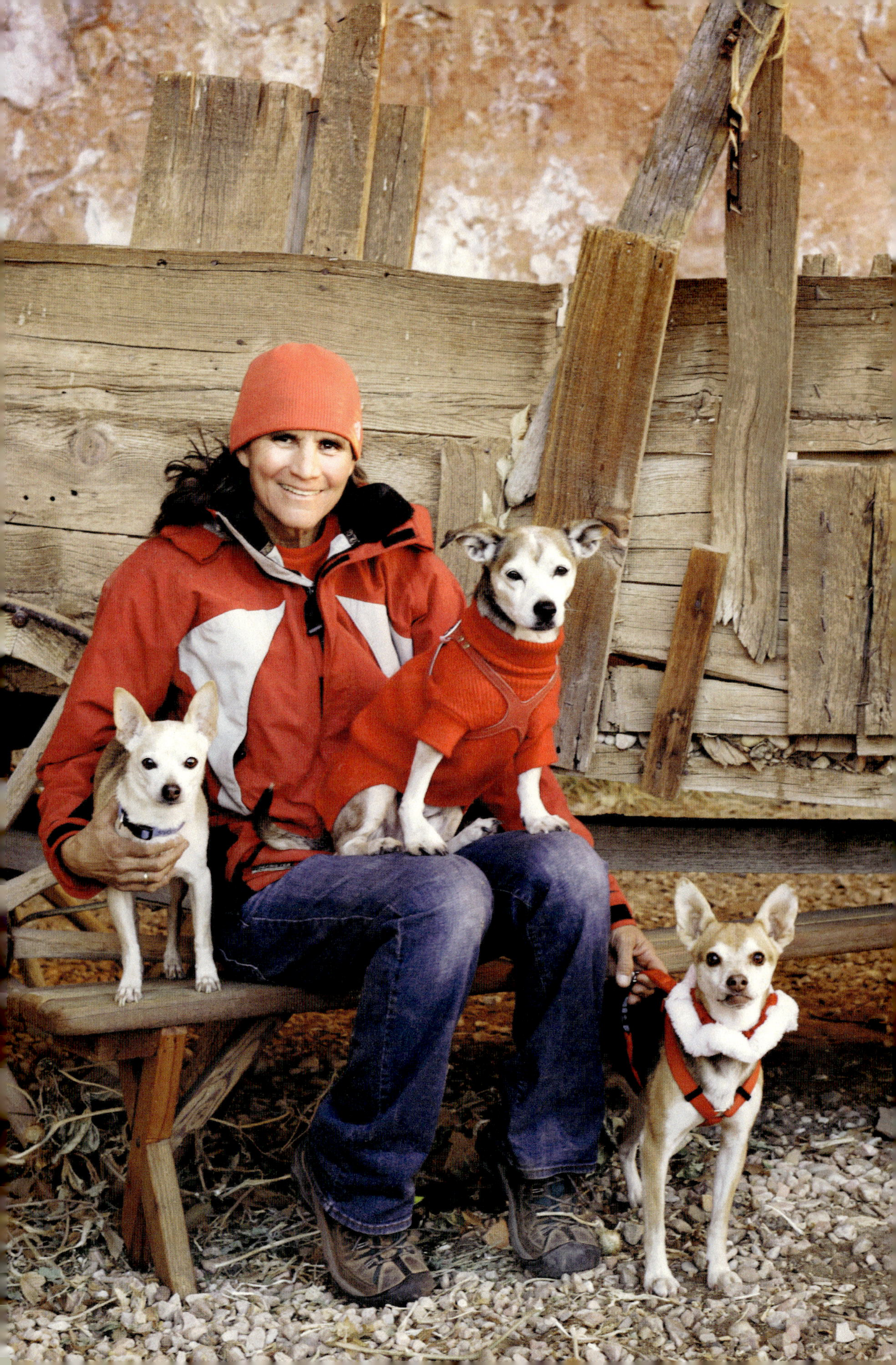

A legacy of love

In 1980, I closed the door on my omnivorous way of life, inspired by the older world-class long-distance runners who embraced a leaner, meaner agrarian aesthetic. My intention was to follow in their footsteps. But in hindsight, it was actually my beloved grandmother who sowed the seeds for finding lightness and joy in plant-based living.

Ruth Danford Jones Hartsoe Johnson, aka Grandma, was a pioneering southern Appalachian woman born at the turn of the 20th century. She lived off the land and planted fruit trees and vegetable and flower gardens to sustain her family. Grandma knew every tree, plant and flower by name, as well as their unique healing properties for home remedies. Food was medicine, too! I lived for the cherished weeks every summer when I could be with her. She modeled the good life, and I imbibed every lesson.

"Grocery store" was not in Grandma's vocabulary. Lettuce, okra, cabbage, carrots, turnip greens, watermelons, cantaloupe, onions... You name it. Grandma grew it. The surrounding trees provided fruits for sauces and jams. I learned how to shuck corn, string green beans and slice vine-ripened cucumbers and tomatoes. I learned where potatoes come from and that one potato, slow-roasted over an open fire, could be a satisfying feast.

Giving up meat improved my athletic performance beyond my wildest dreams. Although I never became a world class runner as I once dreamed, I achieved something even better: the knowledge that my choices of what and how I eat serve the greater good of the planet and all sentient beings.

I remain rooted in the lessons Grandma taught in her open-air classroom. I am blessed and honored to carry on her legacy of plant-based living, which is to say, her legacy of love.

Raven
Best Friends employee with Buddy, Dulce and Sage

Main Meals

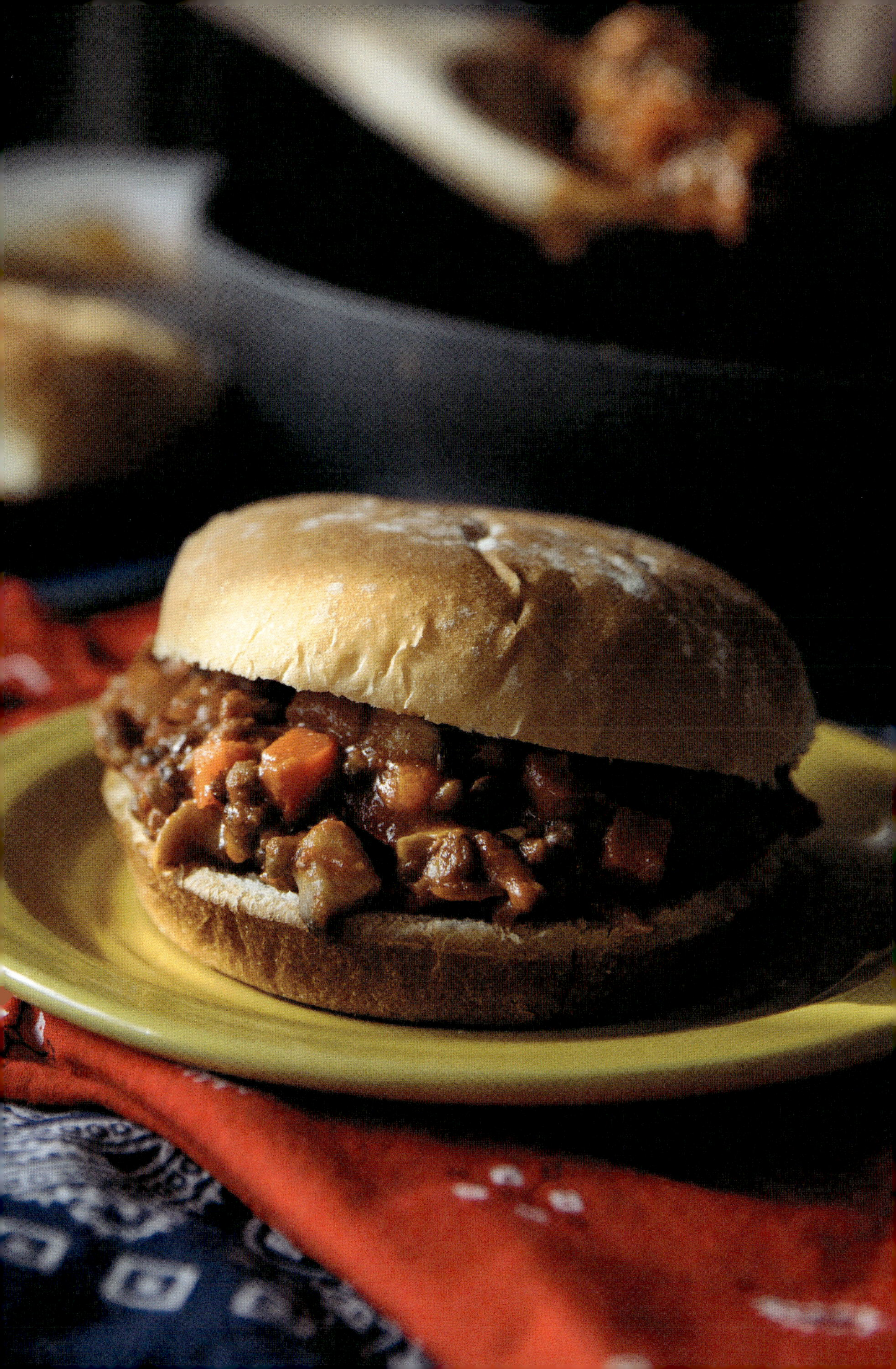

Garden Couscous

Serves 6 to 8

Ingredients

- 1 cup vegetable broth
- 1 cup couscous, uncooked
- 3 cups frozen corn, thawed
- 1 cucumber, diced
- 1½ cup cherry or grape tomatoes, halved
- ½ cup diced red onion
- 1½ cups chickpeas (or 15-ounce can, drained)
- 3 tablespoons olive oil
- 3 tablespoons lemon juice
- 1 teaspoon dried oregano
- ¾ teaspoon ground cumin
- ½ teaspoon salt
- ½ teaspoon ground black pepper
- 3 tablespoons minced fresh parsley

Directions

In a large pot bring broth to a boil and stir in couscous. Remove from heat and let stand 5-10 minutes or until liquid is absorbed. Fluff with a fork.

Transfer the couscous to a large bowl. Stir in the corn, cucumber, tomatoes and red onion.

In a small bowl, whisk together oil, lemon juice and seasonings. Pour over the top of the couscous and veggies and stir until everything is coated. Stir in the herbs.

Serve cold or at room temperature.

Notes

MAINS

Feeling creative? Use cilantro, basil, scallions or dill in place of parsley. Make it gluten-free by replacing the couscous with 3 cups cooked quinoa or millet. Use black beans, edamame or other beans of choice in place of chickpeas. Add grilled tofu or tempeh. Make it a salad by scooping the couscous onto a bed of leafy greens.

'Cheeseburger' Penne

Serves 4

Ingredients

8 ounces penne pasta, or other pasta of choice

1 tablespoon oil

½ cup diced yellow onion

1 cup chopped mushrooms

8 ounces tempeh, crumbled

1 tablespoon vegan Worcestershire sauce

1 tablespoon tamari

1 cup chopped zucchini

15-ounce can diced tomatoes, undrained

½ cup chopped dill pickles

½ teaspoon ground black pepper

½ cup cashew "cheez" sauce, see page 87

Yellow mustard, to taste (optional)

DIY Parmesan (optional, see page 40)

Notes

Feeling creative? Use meatless burger crumbles instead of tempeh. Short on time? Replace the ½ cup of cashew "cheez" with 1 cup of nondairy cheese shreds. Stir leafy greens, such as spinach or kale into the sautéed veggies and tempeh. For Greek-themed, replace pickles with olives, or for Mexican-themed, add 4-ounce can of mild green chiles and a tablespoon of taco seasoning.

Directions

In a large skillet, heat oil over medium-high heat and sauté onions and mushrooms, cooking until onions are translucent, about 3-5 minutes. Add the crumbled tempeh and cook until slightly browned, about 5-7 minutes. Add in the Worcestershire sauce and tamari, stirring until well combined. You may need to add 1 to 2 tablespoons of water to deglaze the pan if the tempeh starts to stick. Next add the zucchini, tomatoes (with their juices), pickles and black pepper, cooking until bubbly. When done, turn off the heat and add the pasta to the veggie/tempeh mixture, folding everything together.

Lightly spray a 9-by-9-inch baking dish with oil and add half of the pasta mixture to the dish. Top the pasta with half of the cashew "cheez," then layer on the other half of the pasta. Drizzle the remaining cashew "cheez" over the top. Cover with foil and bake for 20 minutes.

Serve into bowls and top with a little yellow mustard and DIY Parmesan, if desired.

MAINS

White Bean Stew

Serves 3-4

Ingredients

1 tablespoon oil

½ onion, diced

2 carrots, diced

1 medium potato, diced

2 cups vegetable broth

15-ounce canned white beans, drained and rinsed

½ teaspoon dried oregano

½ teaspoon dried thyme

½ teaspoon salt, plus more to taste (if needed)

Ground pepper, to taste

2 tablespoons tomato paste

2 cups kale, ribs removed and leaves chopped (Dogs love the ribs!)

1 tablespoon lemon juice

Directions

In a large pot, heat the oil over medium-high heat and sauté the onions and carrots for 6-8 minutes.

Add the potatoes, vegetable broth, beans, seasonings and tomato paste, and stir to combine. Bring to a boil, then reduce heat to a simmer and cook for 15 minutes or until potatoes are tender.

Stir in the kale and cook until tender before removing from heat. Stir in the lemon juice, and serve.

Feeling creative? Add some crumbled and browned meatless sausage for an even heartier stew. Substitute another leafy green for the kale. **Pro tip:** Spinach cooks quickly. Swiss chard takes a little longer. And kale takes the longest.

Moussaka

Serves 6 to 8

(This is a time-intensive recipe with multiple components but it will wow your friends and family. If you're short on time, or want to skip the eggplant, you can easily turn this into a shepherd's pie.)

Ingredients

2 eggplants

Salt

Olive oil

Mashed potatoes

3 russet potatoes, peeled (optional) and cubed

3 tablespoons nondairy butter

½ cup unsweetened and unflavored nondairy milk

Salt and pepper

Bechamel sauce

2 tablespoons nondairy butter

2 tablespoons flour

1¼ cups unsweetened and unflavored nondairy milk

¼ cup nutritional yeast

1 teaspoon salt

Pepper to taste

Filling

2 cups sliced mushrooms

1 cup diced onion

15-ounce can diced tomatoes

1 tablespoon red wine vinegar

½ teaspoon garlic powder

½ teaspoon salt

1 teaspoon paprika

1 teaspoon ground cumin

¼ teaspoon ground nutmeg

¼ teaspoon allspice

¼ teaspoon ground ginger

Pinch of ground cloves

15-ounce can of lentils, drained and rinsed (or 2 cups homemade lentils)

Feeling creative? Skip the eggplant and bechamel and make it a shepherd's pie instead! Use a package of meatless beef crumbles or sausage instead of lentils. Sauté your favorite leafy greens with the mushrooms and onions. You could also use quick mashed potato flakes in a pinch to save time instead of making your own mashed potatoes.

MAINS

Directions

Lightly oil a large baking sheet (or line it with parchment paper). Slice both eggplants lengthwise into ½-inch-thick slices and arrange in a single layer on the baking sheet. Season eggplant generously with salt and let sit for 30 minutes. This will draw out moisture and produce beads of water on top of the eggplant.

Meanwhile, in a large pot boil potatoes until tender (15-20 minutes, depending on the size of your pieces). Drain, then transfer to a bowl. Add the vegan butter, milk, salt and pepper and mash with a potato masher or fork. Set aside.

Preheat the oven to 425 degrees F. Remove the beads of water and salt off of the eggplant by patting them with a towel. Drizzle the eggplant with olive oil and roast for 15 minutes or until soft and golden. Remove the eggplant and set aside but keep the oven on.

In a large skillet, sauté the onions and mushrooms over medium-high heat until the onions are translucent and the mushrooms are soft, about 6-8 minutes. Add the rest of the filling ingredients to the pan and cook over low heat until bubbly.

Meanwhile, in a smaller sauce pot, make the bechamel sauce. Melt the butter on medium heat and whisk in the flour. While continuously whisking, slowly add in the milk until the sauce thickens. Finish by adding nutritional yeast, salt and pepper. Whisk until smooth and remove from heat.

Lightly oil a large baking dish and start assembling your moussaka. First add a layer of cooked eggplant slices followed by a layer of the filling and then another layer of eggplant, then filling and, finally, mashed potatoes. Pour the bechamel sauce over the top. Cover with foil and bake for 20 minutes. Remove the foil and bake another 10 minutes or until the top is golden brown.

Notes

MAINS

Feeling creative? Swap the tempeh for a can of chickpeas (drained and rinsed) or 8 ounces of chopped seitan. For more nutrition, add broccoli or cauliflower florets to sauté along with the onion and pepper.

Thai Tempeh in Peanut Sauce

Serves 4

Ingredients

- 1 tablespoon oil
- 1 onion, thinly sliced
- 1 medium red bell pepper, thinly sliced
- 1 medium clove garlic, minced
- 8 ounces tempeh, cut into cubes
- 8 ounces mushrooms, sliced
- ½ cup chopped peanuts (shelled)
- ½ cup unsweetened peanut butter
- 2 cups water
- 3 tablespoons soy sauce or reduced-sodium tamari
- 2 teaspoons cornstarch, whisked and dissolved in ⅔ cup cold water
- 1 tablespoon Sriracha or hot sauce of choice, optional
- Juice of half a lime, plus more if desired
- ¼ cup chopped scallions or cilantro, for garnish

Directions

Sauté onion and red pepper in olive oil over medium-high heat in a large stovetop pan until the onions are translucent, about 3 minutes. Add the garlic and tempeh. Cook until the tempeh begins to brown, stirring frequently and adding 1 to 2 tablespoons of water as needed to deglaze the pan. Once the tempeh is browned, add the mushrooms and cook for an additional 5 minutes or until mushrooms are softened and browned.

Add the peanuts, peanut butter, water, soy sauce or tamari, cornstarch in water and Sriracha (if using). Bring to a boil, then reduce heat and simmer for 15 minutes or until sauce is thickened. Squeeze in lime juice and top with scallions or cilantro.

Serve over rice, Asian noodles or roasted sweet potatoes.

Notes

Pasta with Sausage and Kale

Serves 4

Ingredients

Sauce

14-ounce can of white beans, such as cannellini or great northern (or 1½ cups homemade white beans). Do not drain.

1 teaspoon salt, plus more to taste

2 tablespoons lemon juice

Pasta

8 ounces penne or bowtie pasta

Meatless sausage

4 plant-based brats or plant-based Italian sausages, cut into ½ inch pieces

Kale

6 kale leaves, ribs removed (Dogs love them!) and leaves chopped

1 tablespoon olive oil

1 teaspoon garlic powder

½ teaspoon red pepper flakes, optional

¼ cup toasted pine nuts, optional for garnish

Directions

Transfer the can of beans (liquid included) into a blender with the salt and lemon juice, and puree until smooth. Go for a creamy sauce consistency. If you're using homemade white beans, you can add water or vegetable broth to reach the desired consistency.

Prepare pasta in a large pot according to the package instructions. Drain the pasta, reserving one cup of the pasta water. Return pasta to the pot and add the bean puree, stirring to combine.

Meanwhile, in a large skillet, sauté the sausage over medium heat, turning a few times until the sausage begins to brown. Add the sausage and any drippings to the pasta pot.

In the sausage skillet, sauté the kale on medium heat and cover with a lid. Cook for 3-5 minutes, adding 1 to 2 tablespoons of water as needed to deglaze the pan. Sprinkle garlic powder and red pepper flakes (if using) over the kale and turn occasionally. Keep covered.

Once the kale is tender, transfer it to the pasta and turn the heat on low. Toss to mix everything together. If the mixture looks too dry, add reserved pasta water, ¼ cup at a time. Serve into 4 dishes and top each with a tablespoon of toasted pine nuts.

Notes

MAINS

Feeling creative? To make it more nutritious, use legume or whole-grain pasta and substitute crumbled tempeh in place of meatless sausage. Use spinach instead of kale.

BBQ Jackfruit

Serves 4

Ingredients

20-ounce can of jackfruit, drained and rinsed*

1 tablespoon oil

1 cup diced red onion

2 medium cloves garlic, minced

12-ounce canned tomato sauce

½ cup water

¼ cup packed brown sugar

¼ cup molasses

1 tablespoon chili powder

1 tablespoon apple cider vinegar

½ teaspoon liquid smoke (optional)

Salt and pepper to taste

*The jackfruit should be canned in water or brine, not syrup.

Notes

Directions

Start by shredding the jackfruit. To do this, tear the jackfruit pieces one by one, separating and smashing them between your fingers. Alternatively, you can tear them apart with a fork. The jackfruit will look like pulled pork. Set aside.

In a large pot, heat oil and sauté the onions until lightly brown and soft, about 3-5 minutes, then add the garlic and cook for another minute. Add the tomato sauce, water, sugar, molasses and chili powder. Whisk until smooth. Add the jackfruit and stir to coat. Cover and cook over medium heat for about 40 minutes, stirring occasionally, until the jackfruit is tender and the liquid has thickened. Add apple cider vinegar, liquid smoke (if using), and salt/pepper to taste.

Serve on a bun (à la sloppy joes) or skip the bun and make it a hearty salad. The options are endless!

Feeling creative? If you prefer less sugar, reduce the brown sugar and molasses by 25%. Add some chili powder and use for tacos, burritos or as nacho topping.

MAINS

Tamale Pie

Makes one 9-by-13-inch casserole

Ingredients

1 tablespoon oil

1 cup onion, diced

1 medium red bell pepper, diced

1 medium green bell pepper, diced

1 zucchini, diced

15-ounce can black beans, drained and rinsed (or 1½ cups homemade black beans)

15-ounce canned diced tomatoes

2 teaspoons minced garlic

1 teaspoon salt

1 tablespoon mild chili powder (or less, if yours is very spicy)

1 teaspoon ground cumin

½ teaspoon ground coriander

Pinch of cayenne (optional)

1 batch of cornbread batter

Cornbread batter

2 cups flour

¼ cup sugar

1 cup cornmeal

½ teaspoon salt

½ tablespoon baking powder

½ cup oil

1½ cups nondairy milk or water

1½ tablespoon vinegar

½ cup frozen or fresh corn

Feeling creative? To make your tamale pie more nutritious, use oat flour or whole wheat flour in place of white flour, and coconut sugar in place of white sugar. Use masa harina in place of cornmeal or substitute ½ cup unsweetened applesauce to make the cornbread oil-free.

Directions

Preheat oven to 350 degrees F.

In a large skillet, heat oil over medium heat and sauté onions and peppers. When they start to soften (after about 3-5 minutes), add the zucchini and cook 2-3 minutes longer until zucchini is lightly browned but not too soft.

Add in all remaining ingredients except the cornbread batter, stirring to combine. Taste for seasoning, adding additional salt or spices as desired. Pour the mixture into an oiled baking dish and set aside.

To make the cornbread batter, combine all dry ingredients in a large bowl and mix well. In a separate bowl or large measuring cup, combine all liquid ingredients. Slowly add the liquid to the dry ingredients and stir with a spatula until well-combined and no powder clumps remain. Fold in the corn. Spoon the batter over the veggies in the baking dish, spreading it out evenly. Bake the tamale pie for 30 minutes or until the cornbread is cooked through and golden brown.

MAINS

Korean Street Tacos

Serves 4

Ingredients

- 1 large head cauliflower, cut into bite-size florets
- 2 tablespoons oil
- 1 teaspoon garlic powder
- ¼ cup reduced-sodium soy sauce or tamari
- ½ cup sweet chili sauce
- 1 teaspoon rice vinegar
- 1 tablespoon brown sugar or coconut sugar
- ¼ cup sliced green onions
- 4-8 tortillas, depending on size

Directions

Preheat oven to 425 degrees F and oil a large baking sheet or line it with parchment paper. Toss the cauliflower in a large bowl with oil until the pieces are coated. Season with garlic powder. Arrange in a single layer on the baking sheet. Roast for about 15 minutes or until cauliflower starts to brown.

While the cauliflower is roasting, make the sauce. In a pot over medium-high heat, whisk together the soy sauce or tamari, sweet chili sauce, vinegar and brown sugar. Bring the sauce to a boil, stirring often, and cook until slightly thickened (about 2-3 minutes). Remove from heat and set aside.

When cauliflower is done, transfer it back into the bowl and pour the sauce over the top, tossing gently to coat. Spoon into warmed tortillas and top with green onions.

Notes

MAINS

Feeling creative? For the tortillas, use any you prefer (flour, corn, whole-grain or sprouted grain and seed). As an option, you can substitute lettuce wraps, collard greens or Swiss chard in place of tortillas. You can add some chopped leafy greens such as arugula or spinach into your taco. Spread a little vegan mayo on the tortilla before filling and top the cauliflower with kimchi, veggie sprouts and sesame seeds for more nutrition!

Feeling creative? Use tofu or tempeh instead of meatless chicken. Add bean sprouts or alfalfa sprouts to the lettuce wraps for more nutrition. Try cabbage or collard leaves instead of lettuce for extra crunch.

Cashew Lettuce Wraps

Serves 2-3

Ingredients

1 10-ounce package meatless chicken strips

1 tablespoon oil

½ cup diced yellow onion

½ cup shredded carrots

2 teaspoons minced garlic

½ cup raw cashews

½ cup shredded purple cabbage

1 cup cooked quinoa

1 head butter lettuce, rinsed and separated into pieces for the wraps

Chopped cilantro or parsley (to taste)

Sliced green onions (to taste)

Sauce

¼ cup soy sauce or reduced-sodium tamari

2 tablespoons rice vinegar

2 tablespoons brown sugar or coconut sugar

½ teaspoon ginger powder

1 tablespoon toasted sesame oil

Directions

In a bowl, whisk together all the sauce ingredients until the sugar dissolves, then set aside.

In a large stovetop skillet, cook the meatless chicken according to package instructions. Remove from skillet, let cool slightly, and dice. Set aside.

In the now empty skillet, heat the oil on medium-high heat. Add the onions and carrots, cooking for 3-5 minutes over medium heat or until onions are soft and translucent. Turn the heat down to medium, add the garlic and cook for an additional minute. Stir in the sauce and cashews and cook an additional 4-6 minutes. Add the diced chicken, cabbage and quinoa, stirring to combine before removing from the heat. Let cool slightly before spooning into lettuce wraps. Add chopped herbs like cilantro or parsley and sliced green onion to taste.

Notes

MAINS

Feeling creative? For added nutrition, use whole-grain buns; or instead of a bun, serve your sloppy joes on top of baked or mashed potatoes. For lower carbs, enjoy over wilted dark greens such as swiss chard or spinach. Yum!

Super Sloppy Joes

Makes about 4 large sandwiches

Choose your own adventure with these sloppy joes! Go traditional with meatless beef crumbles (such as Gardein or Beyond Meat), totally plant-powered with lentils and mushrooms, or try old-school vegan with textured vegetable protein (TVP), which is available at natural food stores. Whatever you choose, this quick and easy dinner will be ready in no time.

Ingredients

- 1 tablespoon olive oil
- 1 cup finely diced onion
- 1 medium red bell pepper, finely diced

Protein of choice (pick one):
- 1 package meatless beef crumbles (These can vary in size from 12 to 16 ounces.)
- 1 15-ounce can lentils (drained and rinsed), plus 8 ounces chopped mushrooms
- 2 cups dry TVP rehydrated with 1½ cups boiling water

- 1 medium clove garlic, minced
- 15-ounce can of tomato sauce
- 1 to 2 tablespoons chili powder (depending on heat and personal taste)
- 2 tablespoons soy sauce or reduced-sodium tamari
- 1 tablespoon Dijon mustard
- Salt and pepper to taste
- 4 large hamburger buns

Directions

Heat a large skillet over medium heat, add the olive oil and sauté onions, peppers and garlic until onions are soft and translucent, about 3-5 minutes.

If you're using lentils and mushrooms, add the mushrooms to the pepper and onion mixture and sauté until softened, about 5-8 minutes, before adding the lentils. Cook until lentils are heated through, about 5 minutes.

If you're using beef crumbles or rehydrated TVP, add them to the pepper and onion mixture. Sauté for 5-7 minutes or until beef crumbles are thawed and cooked, or the TVP has browned.

Add tomato sauce, chili powder, soy sauce or tamari and mustard. If the mixture becomes too dry, add a couple of tablespoons of water at a time to keep everything cooking without burning. Simmer for about 5 more minutes, add salt and pepper to taste (if needed). Serve on hamburger buns. Don't forget the napkins!

Notes

MAINS

Bark Mi: Best Friends Bánh Mì

Serves 4

Our spin on the bánh mì sandwich pairs meatballs or mushrooms with pickled veggies and slaw in a toasted hoagie bun. You might be a little apprehensive about the sauce, but trust us. It works!

Ingredients

1 package meatless meatballs or 16 ounces thin-sliced portobello mushrooms

4 hoagie rolls or small baguettes

Pickled veggies

½ cup red onion, thinly sliced

½ cup carrot, julienned or grated

½ cup cucumber, thinly sliced

½ cup white vinegar

½ cup water

2 tablespoons sugar

1 teaspoon salt

Sauce

¼ cup sweet chili sauce

¼ cup grape jelly

Slaw

4 cups coleslaw mix

2 tablespoons egg-free mayo, plus more for spreading on rolls

1 teaspoon Sriracha (optional), plus more to taste

Juice of half a lime

Pinch of salt

Directions

Make the pickled veggies first. Slice the veggies, combine them in a jar and set aside. In a small pot, combine the water, vinegar, sugar and salt, and bring to a boil. Remove from the heat and carefully pour into the jar of veggies. Lid the jar, and let cool for at least 30 minutes before using the veggies or place the jar of veggies in the fridge for later. You may have some leftover pickled veggies, which will last for a week in the fridge.

Meanwhile, make your slaw. Add the 2 tablespoons of mayo, Sriracha (can be omitted if you don't like spicy food), lime juice and salt to the coleslaw mix, and stir until well combined. Set aside.

Cook the meatballs according to the package directions, then let them cool enough to slice in half. (This will prevent them from rolling out of your sandwich.) If you're using mushrooms, sauté them over medium-high heat with a tablespoon of olive oil, until browned. Whisk the sweet chili sauce with the grape jelly, and then add this sauce to the meatballs or mushrooms in a pan on medium-low heat for a couple of minutes until it's bubbly and hot. Remove from the heat and let it sit for 5 minutes to allow the sauce to thicken even more.

Slice the hoagie rolls lengthwise and toast them. Spread some mayo on each roll (if desired), divide the bánh mì filling among the four sandwiches, add some pickled veggies and top it all off with the slaw. Or you can serve your slaw on the side if that's how you roll. Add more Sriracha for a hot kick. Then, close up the sandwich and devour it like a dog whose person just left a pizza unattended!

MAINS

Feeling creative? This recipe tastes great with baked tofu, seitan or almost any plant-based meat. Up the nutritional punch of your slaw by using broccoli slaw instead of cabbage. Switch up your pickled veggies by adding thinly sliced radishes, jalapenos or whatever else you like, for 1½ cups total of mixed veggies. Gluten-free? Ditch the hoagie roll for a gluten-free wrap.

Mushroom Stroganoff

Serves 4

Ingredients

16 ounces bowtie pasta or pasta of your choice

2 tablespoons oil

1½ cups diced yellow onion

16 ounces mushrooms (any kind), chopped

2 medium cloves garlic, minced

2 tablespoons flour

1 cup vegetable broth

½ teaspoon paprika

1 teaspoon Dijon mustard

1 teaspoon vegan Worcestershire sauce

¼ cup nondairy sour cream or cream cheese

1 to 3 teaspoons lemon juice (depending on how sour your sour cream is)

Salt and pepper to taste

Directions

Cook pasta according to package directions. Drain the pasta, return it to the pot and drizzle with one tablespoon of oil, then set aside.

Meanwhile, in a large skillet, add the other tablespoon of oil and the onions. Sauté for 3-5 minutes over medium heat. Add mushrooms and garlic and sauté for another 5-10 minutes until mushrooms release their liquid and are browned.

Add in flour, stir to coat and cook for a minute or two, being careful not to burn the flour. Slowly add in broth and whisk until combined. Reduce heat and simmer, stirring frequently until thickened.

Stir in paprika, mustard, sour cream or cream cheese, lemon juice, salt and pepper. Add the mushrooms and sauce to the pasta. Stir to combine.

Notes

Feeling creative? For a protein boost, add a bag of plant-based beef crumbles or crumbled tempeh with the mushrooms. To make it more nutritious, use legume or whole-grain pasta. Use unsweetened, unflavored nondairy yogurt in place of sour cream or cream cheese.

Chimichurri Enchiladas

Serves 4 to 6

Ingredients

2 tablespoons oil, divided

1 medium sweet potato, peeled (optional) and diced (about 3 cups)

1 cup diced yellow onion

1 medium zucchini, diced

15-ounce canned black beans, drained (or 1½ cups precooked beans)

20-ounce canned green enchilada sauce

8 to 12 8-inch flour tortillas

Half batch of cashew "cheez" sauce (page 87) or 1 cup shredded nondairy cheese

Chimichurri

1 cup cilantro

1 cup parsley

¼ cup olive oil

¼ cup red wine vinegar

2 teaspoons minced garlic

½ teaspoon salt

¼ teaspoon red pepper flakes, optional

Directions

Preheat the oven to 400 degrees F. In a large bowl, toss the sweet potatoes with a tablespoon of oil and spread evenly onto a parchment-lined baking sheet. Sprinkle with a pinch of salt, then roast in the oven for 15 minutes or until tender but not mushy.

Meanwhile, heat a large skillet over medium heat. Add the remaining tablespoon of oil and the onions and sauté until translucent, about 3-5 minutes. Add the zucchini and sauté an additional 2-3 minutes, before stirring in the black beans. Cook for another 4-5 minutes, just to heat the beans.

Remove the sweet potatoes from the oven and transfer them back into the large bowl. Turn the oven down to 375 degrees F and add the black bean veggie mixture to the sweet potatoes. Gently toss together. Set aside.

To make the chimichurri, add all the ingredients to a blender and blend until smooth. Alternatively, you can finely mince the cilantro, parsley and garlic, and whisk them together with the other ingredients in a bowl or jar. The texture will be chunkier but it still works. Pour half of the chimichurri sauce into the black bean veggie mixture and fold it in. Set aside the rest of the sauce until you are ready to serve.

Pour half a cup of enchilada sauce into a 9-by-13-inch oiled baking dish, spreading it around the bottom. Then pour the rest of the enchilada sauce into the now empty skillet that you cooked your veggies in. One at a time, take a tortilla, dip it in the enchilada sauce, flip it over and dip again. Add about a half cup of the veggie mixture to each tortilla. Roll them up and place them seam side down in the baking dish. Repeat until you've run out of veggie mixture or room in your dish (after about 8-12 tortillas, depending on how full you stuff them).

Pour remaining enchilada sauce from the pan over the top of the enchiladas, and then drizzle the top with cashew "cheez" sauce (page 87) or vegan cheese shreds.

Bake uncovered at 375 degrees F for 20 minutes or until the cashew "cheez" is golden and slightly firm. If using nondairy cheese shreds, you may want to cover the enchiladas with foil to protect the cheese from drying out. Remove the enchiladas from the oven, serve onto plates and drizzle with additional chimichurri.

> *Feeling creative?* Use red enchilada sauce, or even skip the chimichurri altogether if that's how you roll. It will still taste great! Use diced meatless chicken instead of beans or substitute your favorite veggies for the veggies used in this recipe. Boost the nutrition by adding leafy greens such as spinach or kale to the sautéed veggies, and choose whole-grain or gluten-free tortillas in place of white flour tortillas. For a kick, top the enchiladas with nutritional yeast.

MAINS

'Tuna' Casserole

Serves 4

Ingredients

8 ounces elbow macaroni, or pasta of choice

1 tablespoon oil

14-ounce canned hearts of palm, drained and chopped

1 cup frozen peas, thawed

½ teaspoon Old Bay seasoning or Cajun seasoning

Topping

¼ cup Panko breadcrumbs

2 tablespoons crispy fried onions (optional)*

1 tablespoon chopped cilantro

Sauce

1 medium-size Yukon gold potatoes, diced

½ cup diced carrots

½ cup raw cashews

⅓ cup diced yellow onion

⅓ cup oil

1 teaspoon minced garlic

½ teaspoon mustard from a jar (Dijon is great.)

1 tablespoon lemon juice

1 teaspoon salt

¼ teaspoon ground black pepper

⅛ teaspoon cayenne pepper

Directions

Cook macaroni to al dente according to package directions. Drain, return to pot and drizzle with one tablespoon of oil. Mix in hearts of palm, Old Bay or Cajun-brand seasoning and peas. Set aside.

Meanwhile, combine the potatoes, carrots, cashews and onions in another stovetop pot. Fill it with water, just covering the vegetables. Bring to a boil and cook until the potatoes are fork tender, about 10 minutes.

Preheat oven to 350 degrees F.

Using a slotted spoon, transfer the veggies and cashews to a blender. Add the oil, garlic, mustard, lemon juice, salt, black pepper and cayenne pepper. Blend until smooth, using leftover cooking water to thin the sauce, if needed. Use just enough to keep the blender moving and to make sure the sauce is smooth and creamy without being too runny. Pour the sauce over the noodles and stir to coat evenly. Transfer the pasta to an oiled baking dish, cover with foil and bake 15-20 minutes. Remove foil, top with breadcrumbs and crispy fried onions (if using) and bake an additional 10 minutes. Top with cilantro and serve.

*For the crispy fried onions, you can purchase these prepackaged in many grocery stores or make your own by lightly pan frying onions on your stovetop. They may not be as crispy as the store-bought but they'll still be delicious on top of the casserole!

MAINS

Feeling creative? For more nutrition, use legume or whole-grain pasta. Substitute another type of potato like red or russet in place of Yukon gold. Stir leafy greens like spinach or kale into the casserole mixture before baking.

Pineapple Fried Rice

Serves 4

Ingredients

Rice

1 cup dry rice

¾ cup pineapple chunks (from a can, with ½ cup of juice reserved)

Tofu

14-ounce block extra-firm or firm tofu, drained

Vegetables

4 medium cloves garlic, minced

½ cup peas

½ cup shredded carrots

Sauce

¼ cup soy sauce or reduced-sodium tamari

1 tablespoon peanut butter

2 tablespoons brown sugar

1 clove garlic, minced

1 teaspoon chili garlic sauce

1 teaspoon toasted sesame oil

Topping

½ cup sliced green onions

Directions

Prepare rice according to package directions, except replace ½ cup of water with pineapple juice. Set aside to cool.

Preheat oven to 400 degrees F.

Meanwhile, prepare the tofu by placing it between two clean kitchen towels and gently but firmly pressing out any excess liquid (being careful not to mash your tofu into crumbles). This step is important for your tofu to brown. When the tofu is completely drained of moisture (when no more liquid comes out as you squeeze it), cube the tofu into one-inch pieces and spread it out evenly on a baking sheet lined with parchment paper. Bake for 20 minutes, tossing halfway through, until tofu is golden and crispy. Remove and set aside.

In a medium bowl, whisk all sauce ingredients together until you get a smooth consistency. Transfer the baked tofu to the sauce, stir and allow to marinate.

Meanwhile, heat a large skillet over medium heat, then add the garlic, peas, pineapple chunks and carrots. Season with a splash of soy sauce or tamari. Cook until fragrant and carrots are slightly softened, about 2-3 minutes. Using a slotted spoon, move the tofu to the pan and cook an additional 4-5 minutes, stirring often to prevent sticking. Add the rice to the pan, add the remaining sauce from the bowl and cook for an additional five minutes. Add more soy sauce for seasoning, if desired. Divide between serving dishes and top with sliced green onions.

MAINS

Feeling creative? Use brown, red or black rice in place of white. Add more veggies such as red bell peppers and onions at the beginning of cooking or spinach or kale at the end of cooking. Enjoy!

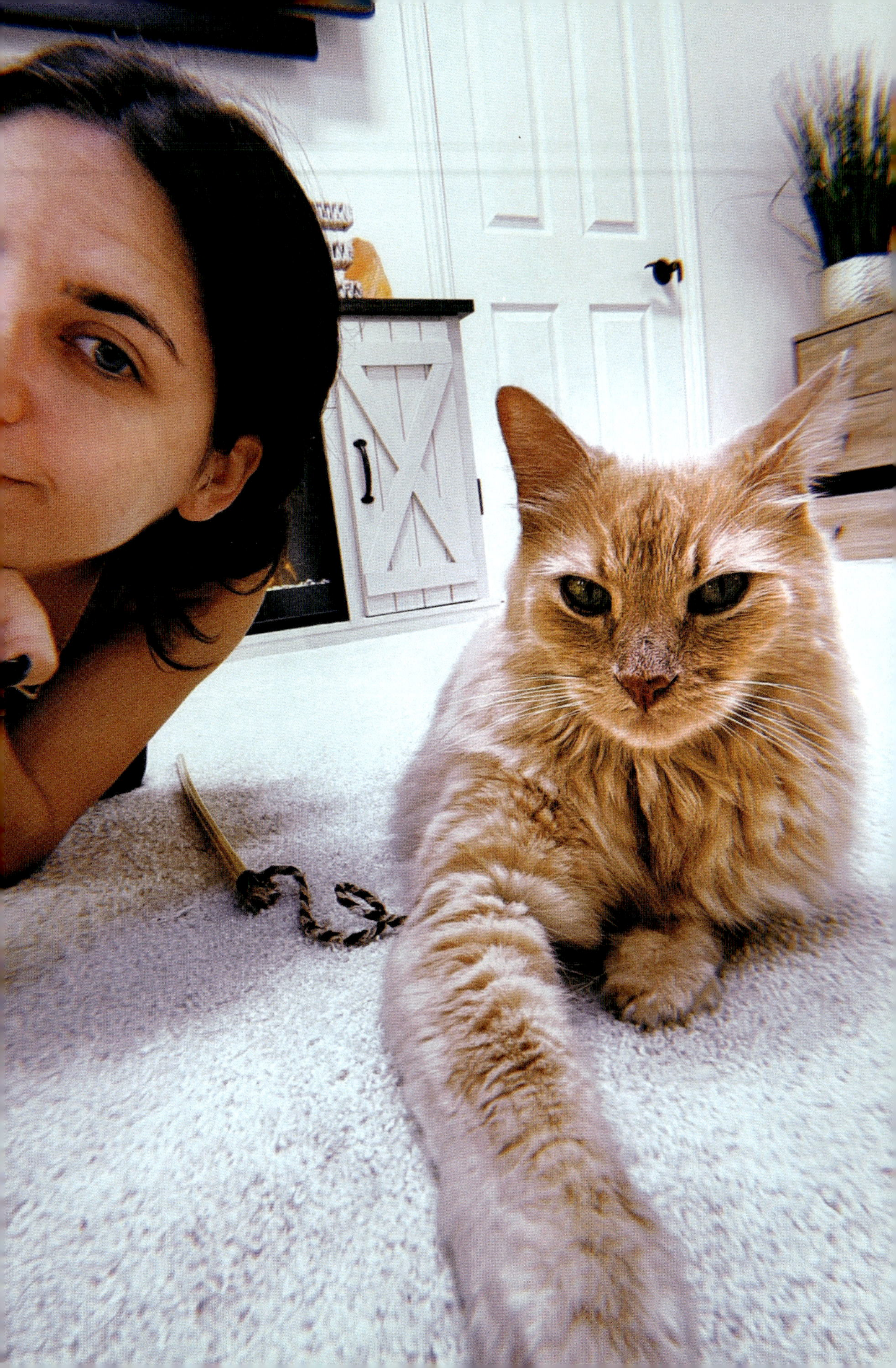

Perfection isn't necessary

I've been an animal lover all my life, but my eating habits didn't always truly align with my values. I bounced around from being a vegetarian to not being a vegetarian for many years. I think it's important to tell people that perfection isn't necessary. Incorporating a plant-based diet in any way you can benefits the animals and environment more than you know.

My cooking skills really blossomed when I became a plant-based eater. Vegans eat more than just salads! I was so fascinated with this new world and was so eager to master it. There are so many alternatives out there and fun ways to make plants taste even better. My favorite things to cook are curries, pastas and savory bowls. Go, nutritional yeast!

Kasey
Best Friends employee with Ketchup

Appetizers, Sides & Sauces

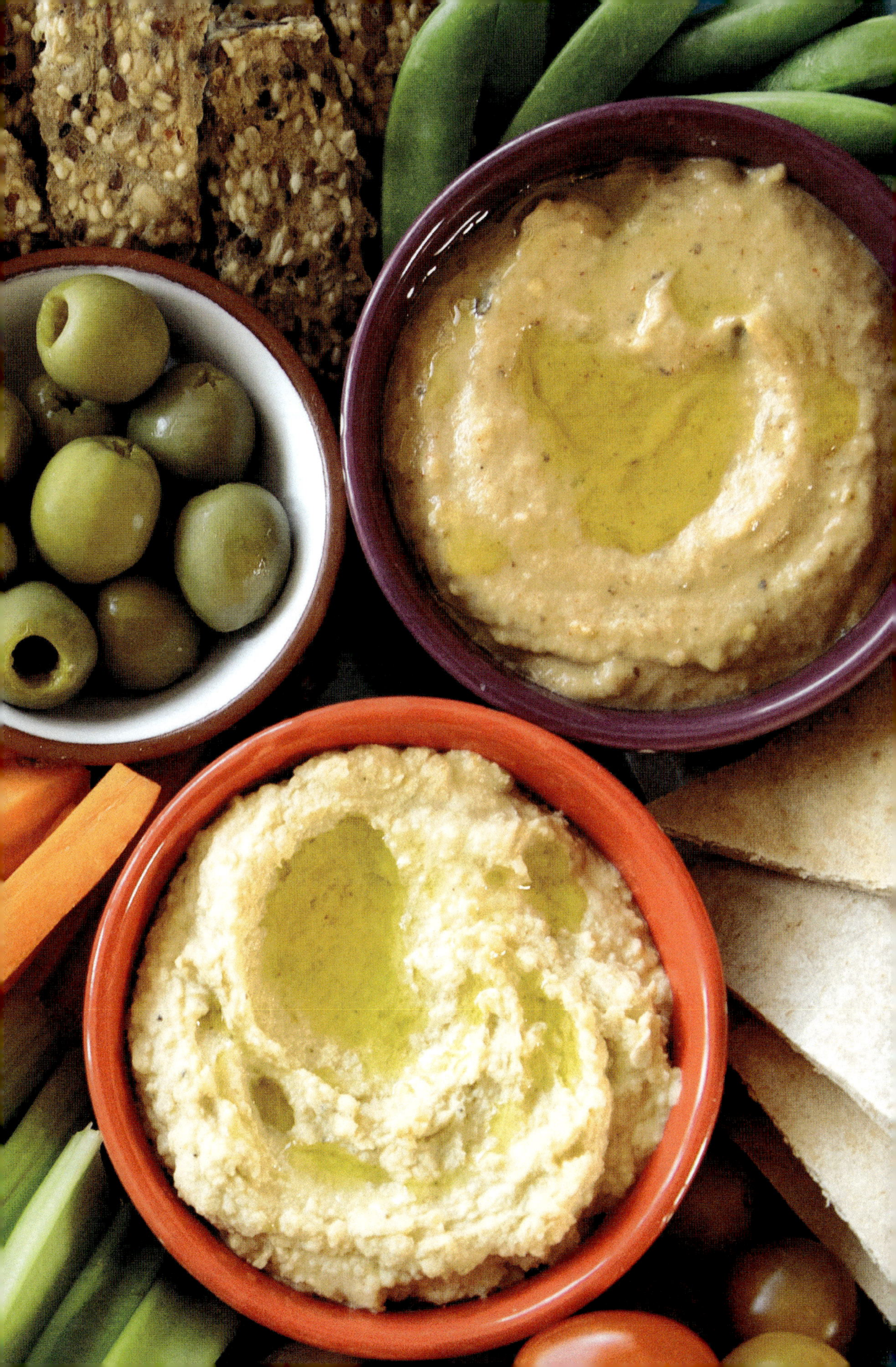

Southwest Medley

Serves 4 to 6

Ingredients

- 1 tablespoon oil
- 1 cup onion, diced
- 1 medium red bell pepper, diced
- 1 jalapeno, seeded and minced, optional
- 2 medium cloves garlic, minced
- 2 medium zucchini or summer squash, diced
- 15-ounce canned black beans, drained and rinsed (or 1½ cups precooked beans)
- 2 cups frozen corn, thawed
- 1 teaspoon ground cumin
- 1 teaspoon ground chili powder (mild or spicy), or more if desired
- ¾ teaspoon salt
- 3 tablespoons lime juice
- ½ cup chopped cilantro
- Salt and pepper to taste

Directions

In a large skillet or pot, heat oil over medium-high heat and sauté the onion, pepper and jalapeno until the veggies become soft and onion is translucent, about 3-5 minutes. Add the garlic and zucchini and cook for 3 minutes more or until zucchini is slightly tender but still crisp. Add the black beans, corn, cumin, chili powder and salt, and cook until the beans and corn are heated through. Remove from heat, add lime juice and cilantro and adjust the seasonings to taste.

Serve the medley hot or cold. You can eat this as a side dish, as a chunky dip with chips, atop a salad, over a bowl of rice or quinoa (with hot sauce) or in tacos.

Notes

APPETIZERS, SIDES & SAUCES

Feeling creative? Use a poblano pepper instead of bell pepper. Add chopped avocado. Use pinto or kidney beans in place of black beans. It's your medley, after all!

Tomato & Avocado 'Caprese' Toast

Serves 4

Ingredients

4 slices rustic Italian bread or other firm, crusty bread

1 avocado

Juice of half a lemon

1 or 2 large heirloom tomatoes, sliced

¼ cup fresh basil

Olive oil

Balsamic vinegar

Salt and pepper

Directions

Cut the avocado in half and remove the pit. With a spoon carefully scoop out each half of the avocado. Place each half flat side down on a cutting board and cut into ¼-inch slices. Set in a small bowl, and drizzle with the lemon juice.

Shred the basil, slicing it into thin ribbons. We like to call this process "chiffonade."

Toast the bread, then drizzle with a little balsamic vinegar and olive oil.

Top each piece of toast with a layer of tomato, a layer of avocado, garnish with basil and dress with more balsamic and olive oil. Sprinkle salt and pepper to taste.

Notes ___

___
___
___
___
___
___
___

APPETIZERS, SIDES & SAUCES

Feeling creative? Use whole-grain or whole-wheat bread for more nutrition. Layer more veggies on top, such as sliced radishes, arugula, sprouts or diced red onion. Buon appetito!

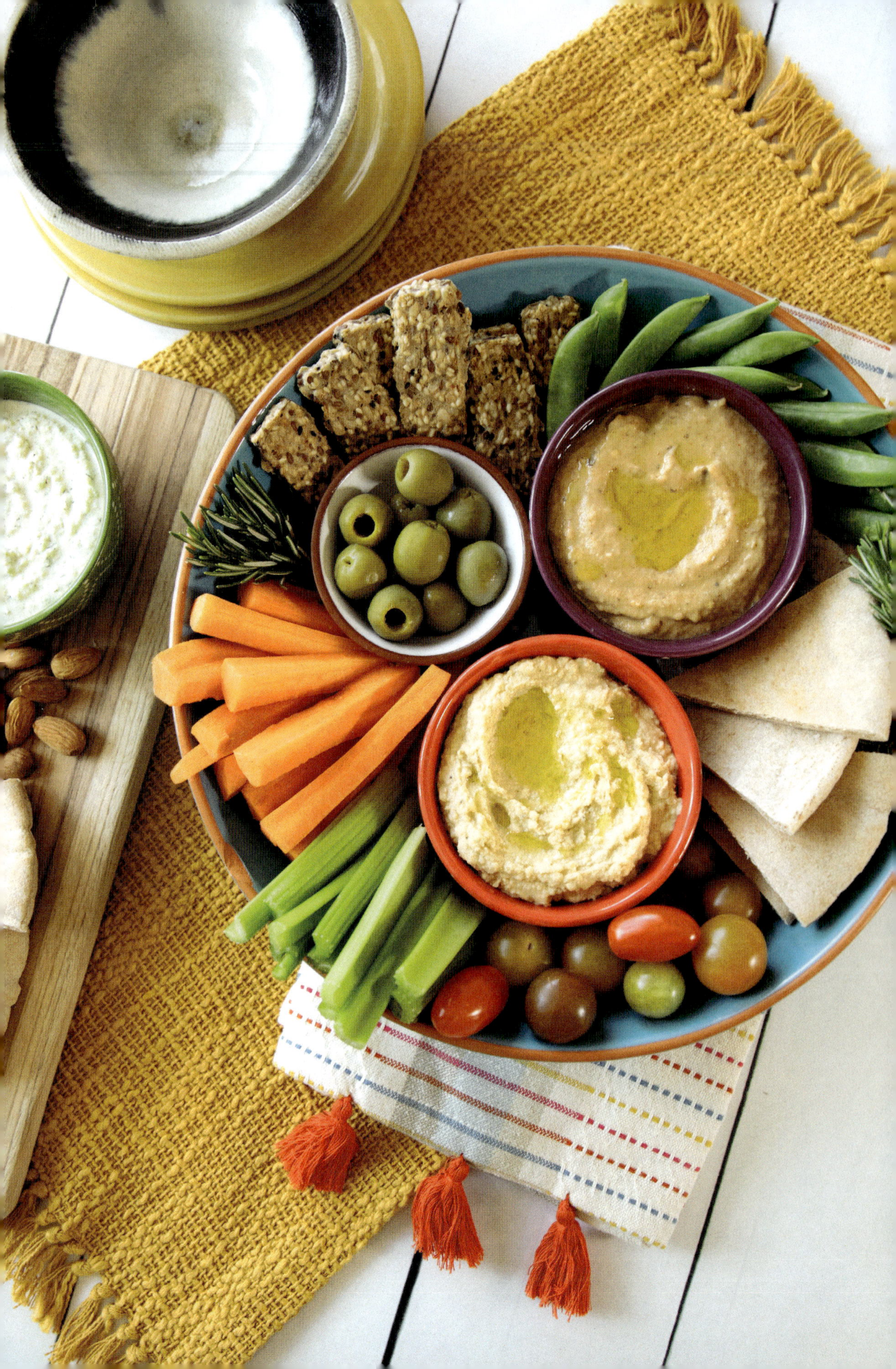

Mediterranean Mezze Platter

In the Mediterranean and the Middle East, mezze means delicious finger foods. At Best Friends, we use these dips and spreads as appetizers on party trays and as great afternoon snacks. It's fun to display the tzatziki, hummus and baba ghanoush in festive bowls and place them on a large cutting board. Then for a flourish, we spread around the board triangle slices of whole grain pita bread, sliced carrots and celery, whole grain crackers, dried fruit, toasted nuts and fresh herbs, such as rosemary. You can also add a bowl of green or black olives (such as Kalamata) and a plate of nondairy cheese spread to the mezze. The options are endless, and we hope you get creative!

Notes

APPETIZERS, SIDES & SAUCES

Baba Ghanoush

Makes about 1½ cups

Ingredients

1 medium eggplant (about 1 pound)

2 tablespoons lemon juice

3 tablespoons tahini

1 tablespoon olive oil

1 teaspoon minced garlic

¼ teaspoon salt

¼ teaspoon smoked paprika, optional (for extra smokiness)

Directions

Preheat the oven to 400 degrees F. Poke the skin of the eggplant in several places with a fork. If you have a gas range, skewer the eggplant and carefully hold it over the medium open flame of the burner until the skin starts to char. This will give it a traditional smoky flavor. (If you don't have a gas range, you can skip this step.) Roast the eggplant directly on oven rack for approximately 60 minutes or until very tender.* Allow eggplant to cool, then cut in half and spoon out the pulp into a bowl. Discard the skin. With a fork or potato masher, mash the eggplant. Stir in the remaining ingredients until well-combined, and adjust flavor to your preference with additional salt and/or lemon juice (if desired). If you want your baba to be silky smooth, you can also pulse it in a food processor. To serve, spread the dip in a shallow bowl and drizzle with additional olive oil, if desired.

*Limited on time? Skip the roasting and microwave the eggplant on high for 7-10 minutes.

Feeling creative? For an extra kick of spice, sprinkle hot pepper flakes on top. Cut pita bread into points and lightly toast to eat with your baba. For fewer carbs, cut up carrots and cucumber to dip.

Notes

APPETIZERS, SIDES & SAUCES

Hummus

Serves 4

Ingredients

1 15-ounce can of chickpeas, drained and rinsed (or 1½ cups homemade chickpeas)

2 tablespoons tahini

2 tablespoons olive oil

2 tablespoons lemon juice

2 teaspoons minced garlic

½ teaspoon salt

¼ teaspoon pepper

1 to 4 tablespoons water, as needed

Garlic hummus: Double the garlic or top with garlic cloves roasted in olive oil.

Roasted red pepper hummus: Add ¼ cup of roasted red peppers. Top with red pepper flakes for some heat. Start with a little and build to your taste.

Herb hummus: Simply mince some herbs such as parsley, basil, cilantro or mint, and sprinkle them on top.

Directions

Add all ingredients except the water to a food processor and mix on low. You may need to scrape the sides occasionally. Switch to high and process for a couple of minutes to get the hummus as smooth as your machine will allow. If necessary, add water (one tablespoon at a time) to keep things moving and make the hummus creamier. It may take several minutes to reach a very smooth consistency. The store-bought varieties you're used to may be creamier but our hummus is every bit as delicious! Serve with olive oil, toasted sunflower seeds or sesame seeds for extra flair.

Tzatziki

Makes about 1 cup

Ingredients

½ cup silken tofu, drained

1 tablespoon olive oil

2 teaspoons minced garlic

1 tablespoon lemon juice

½ teaspoon apple cider vinegar

1 teaspoon minced fresh dill or ¼ teaspoon dried dill

¼ teaspoon salt

⅛ teaspoon ground black pepper

Half of an English cucumber

Directions

In a food processor add all ingredients except the cucumber. Pulse until smooth. Cut the cucumber in half lengthwise, scrape out the seeds and discard. Grate the cucumber and, with clean hands, squeeze out any liquid over the sink. Add the cucumber to the blender and pulse a few times until it is finely chopped and all ingredients are well incorporated. Do not over-blend. The cucumber should still be chunky.

APPETIZERS, SIDES & SAUCES

Stovetop Baked Beans

Serves 4

Ingredients

1 cup diced onion

28-ounce canned pinto beans, drained and rinsed (or 3 cups precooked beans)

5-ounce can of mild, diced green chiles

1 teaspoon vegan Worcestershire sauce

¼ cup ketchup

½ cup brown sugar

1 teaspoon mustard

1 tablespoon molasses or maple syrup

2 teaspoons apple cider vinegar

Directions

In a large pot over medium-high heat, sauté the onion until translucent, about 3-5 minutes. Add the remaining ingredients,stirring until combined. Reduce heat to low, cover and simmer for 25 minutes, until beans are heated through and flavors have combined well.

> *Feeling creative?* Substitute coconut sugar in place of brown sugar or use kidney or black beans in place of pinto beans. Chop up a meatless hot dog for frank and beans. This is comfort food with a sweet kick!

Notes

APPETIZERS, SIDES & SAUCES

Cashews Two Ways

Unlock the power of cashews in your kitchen. If you have a high-speed blender (such as a Vitamix or Blendtec), you can skip soaking or boiling the nuts. This versatile, easy-to-make cream will keep in the refrigerator for five days. Whip up a batch to have on hand.

Vanilla Cashew Cream

We love to use this yummy cashew cream as a topper for pancakes, avocado mousse, and most sweet treats.

Ingredients

1 cup raw cashews, soaked 4 hours or overnight (or boiled for 10 minutes and drained)

½ cup + 2 tablespoons water

1 tablespoon maple syrup

1 teaspoon vanilla extract

Directions

Add all ingredients to a food processor and blend until smooth, scraping the sides of the food processor as necessary until the mixture is creamy. Add 1 to 2 tablespoons of water at a time, if needed, to reach the desired consistency.

Feeling creative? Add a dash of cinnamon or cacao powder to make a variety of flavors.

Cashew 'Cheez' Sauce

When you want cheesy enchiladas or pastas or casseroles, think cashew cream! It will change the way you cook, for good.

Ingredients

1 cup raw cashews, soaked 4 hours or overnight (or boiled for 10 minutes) and drained

½ cup + 2 tablespoons water

2 tablespoons nutritional yeast

½ teaspoon of salt

1 tablespoon lemon juice

Directions

Add all ingredients to a food processor and blend until smooth, scraping the sides as necessary until creamy. Add 1 to 2 tablespoons of water at a time, if needed, to reach the desired consistency.

Feeling creative? Add whole sautéed onions or garlic to the mix. Garlic or onion powder will also do; or add fresh or dried herbs of your choice like dill, chives or rosemary to create herbed cashew "cheez."

APPETIZERS, SIDES & SAUCES

A caring kitchen

Food is one of the finer things in life. I genuinely enjoy preparing and eating it, and it holds a deep social and emotional meaning for me. My grandparents were Great Depression-era, first generation Italian Americans who expressed their love primarily by feeding you. My grandmother spent most of her days in the kitchen, and holidays and family gatherings revolved around food. Meat was always a centerpiece of family meals. Given my love of animals, I made a big change. I became a junk food vegetarian and I got sick as my family predicted. I went back to eating meat briefly but the next time that I stopped, I was armed with my first vegan cookbook and a new appreciation for vegetables. The change has been for good.

My diet will never be perfect but I'm healthy and comfortable with the choices I make. And, if I make food for you, you will know that you are a friend to me — perhaps even family. Thanks, Nana, for giving me the gift of a caring kitchen.

Christelle
Best Friends employee with Rusty

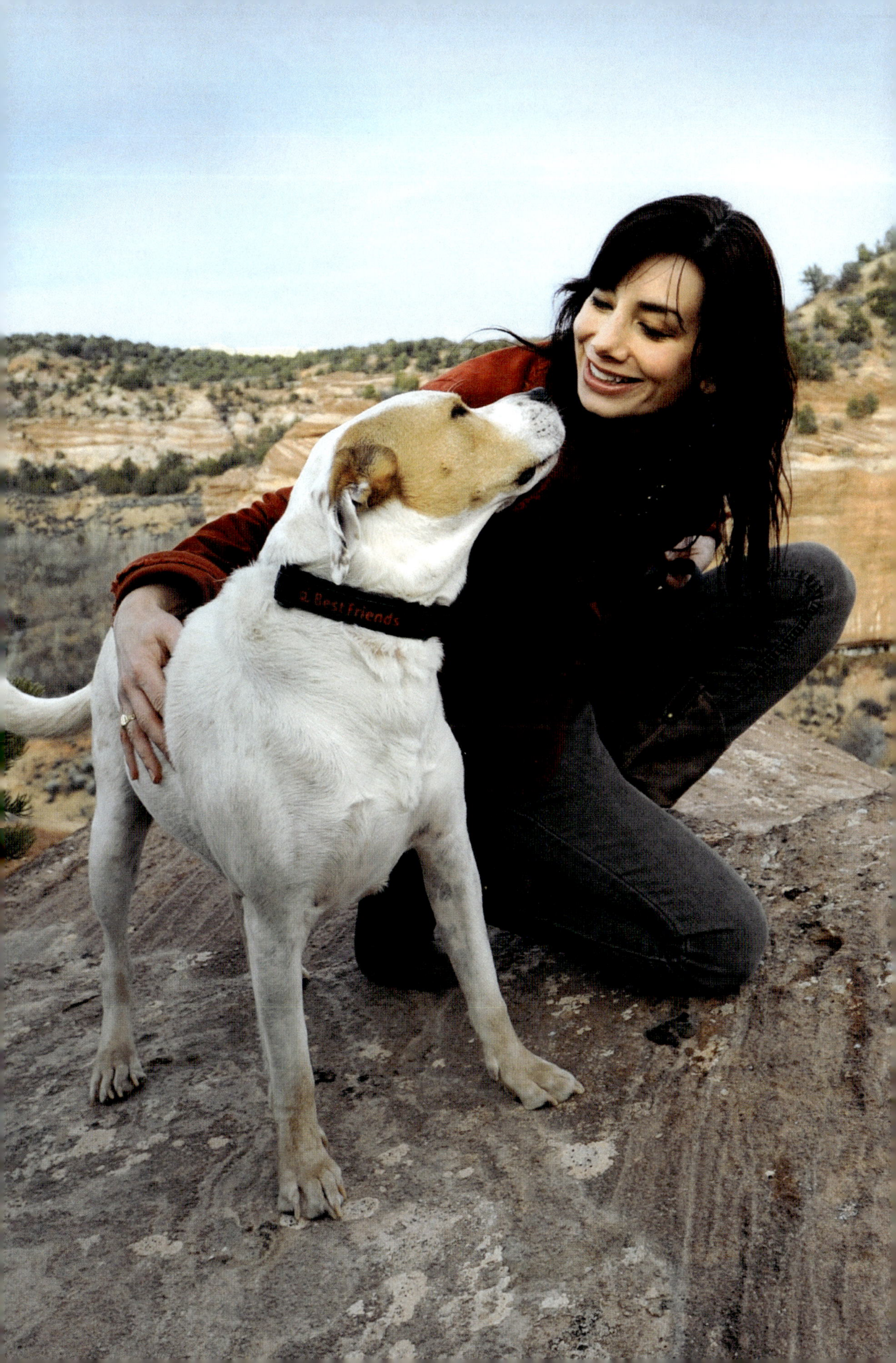
2 Best Friends

Desserts

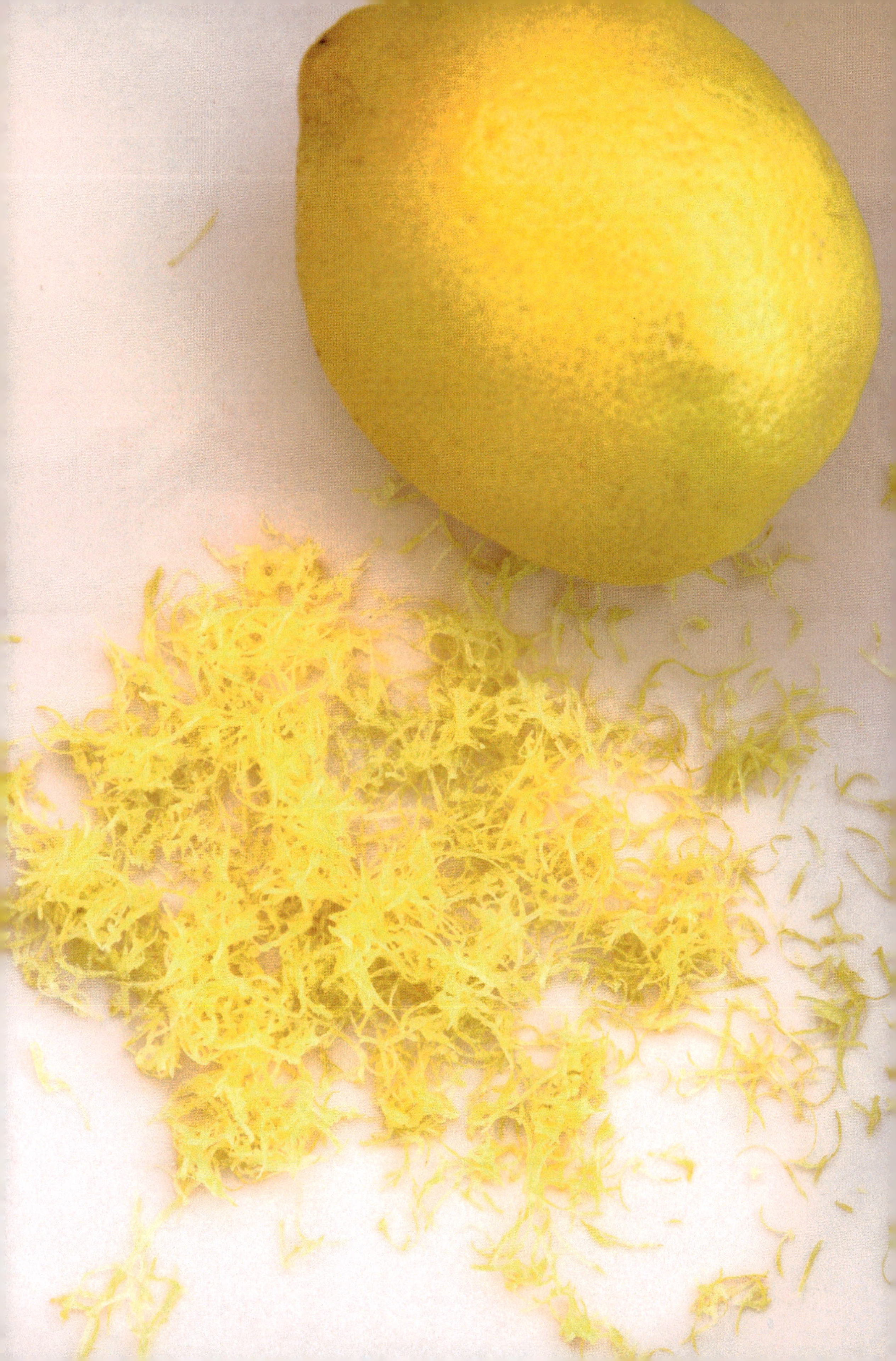

Feeling creative? Add lemon zest for even more lemon flavor. Use lime or orange juice instead of lemon juice for a different flavor profile. Leave out the graham crackers and top with crushed nuts, hemp seeds, flax seeds or pumpkin seeds. Add a teaspoon of a superfood powder such as maca powder or matcha tea.

Lemon Pie Chia Pudding

Serves 2

Ingredients

¼ cup chia seeds

1½ cups nondairy milk

2 tablespoons lemon juice

2 tablespoons maple syrup

¼ cup unsweetened dried shredded coconut

2 pinches salt

Topping

¼ cup crumbled graham crackers

Directions

Add the chia seeds, milk, lemon juice, maple syrup, coconut and salt to a medium-size bowl. Stir so that the ingredients are well-combined and the chia seeds are dispersed evenly throughout the mixture.

Place in refrigerator for 30 minutes, then stir again and let the pudding sit for another 1 to 2 hours before serving. The longer the mixture sits, the more the chia seeds will absorb the liquid and, voilà: A smooth pudding texture is created rather than a crunchy chia seed texture.

Spoon the pudding into two individual bowls and top with crumbled graham crackers.

Notes

___

___

___

___

___

___

DESSERTS

Pumpkin Chocolate Chip Cookies

Makes approximately 24 cookies

Ingredients

1 tablespoon flax meal

3 tablespoons of water

1½ cups flour

½ teaspoon baking soda

½ teaspoon pumpkin pie spice or ground cinnamon

¼ teaspoon salt

½ cup nondairy butter, softened

½ cup brown sugar

¼ cup sugar

½ cup pureed pumpkin

1 teaspoon vanilla extract

1 cup nondairy chocolate chips

Directions

Preheat oven to 350 degrees F and line a baking sheet with parchment paper or lightly spray with oil.

Make your flax "egg" by adding the flax meal and 3 tablespoons of water to a small bowl. Stir and set aside.

In a medium bowl combine the dry ingredients: flour, baking soda, pumpkin pie spice and salt. Mix well.

In a second bowl or stand mixer, cream together butter and both types of sugar until creamy. Add the pureed pumpkin, flax egg and vanilla. Mix for another minute.

Slowly add the flour mixture to the pumpkin mixture and stir until well combined and creamy. The dough will be sticky. Fold in chocolate chips.

Using a cookie scoop or tablespoon, scoop cookies onto the baking sheet 2 inches apart. Bake for 9-12 minutes.

Notes

_____
_____
_____
_____

DESSERTS

Feeling creative? Substitute coconut sugar for white sugar. Instead of the flax "egg," try 1 tablespoon of chia seeds in place of the flax meal, or use 1 tablespoon of egg replacer mixed with 2 tablespoons of water.

Don't stop with peanut butter! Use a variety of nut or seed butters such as cashew, almond or sunflower.

Peanut Butter Cookies

Makes approximately 24 cookies

Peanut butter cookies don't have to be difficult! With just four ingredients, these cookies will melt in your mouth and draw applause.

Ingredients

1 cup peanut butter

1 cup sugar

1 tablespoon flax meal

3 tablespoons water

Directions

Preheat oven to 350 degrees F and line a baking sheet with parchment paper or lightly spray with oil. Make your flax "egg" by adding the flax meal and 3 tablespoons of water to a small bowl. Stir and set aside.

In a large bowl, combine the peanut butter and sugar and mix well by hand or with a hand-held blender. Fold in the flax "egg." That's it, the dough is ready! With a tablespoon, scoop cookies onto the baking sheet and flatten with fork in both directions. (It helps to first dunk the fork in flour to keep it from sticking to the dough.)

Bake for 10-12 minutes or until the bottoms are just golden. Let cool 5 minutes before moving the cookies to a wire rack to cool completely. Pop them into your mouth or crumble them over nondairy ice cream.

Feeling creative? Substitute coconut sugar for white sugar. Instead of the flax "egg," try 1 tablespoon of chia seeds in place of the flax meal, or use 1 tablespoon of egg replacer mixed with 2 tablespoons of water. Don't stop with peanut butter! Make cashew butter cookies or almond butter cookies or sunflower seed cookies by using your chosen type of butter instead of peanut butter.

Notes _____

_____

_____

DESSERTS

PB&C Avocado Mousse with Vanilla Cashew Cream

Serves 4

(That's peanut butter and chocolate if you've never tried it. And oh, you'll be glad when you do!)

Ingredients

2 ripe avocados

¼ cup cocoa powder

¼ cup maple syrup

¼ cup smooth peanut butter (or nut or seed butter of choice)

1 teaspoon vanilla extract

Pinch of salt

4 tablespoons vanilla cashew cream (page 87)

Feeling creative? For a delicious double chocolate mousse, replace the peanut butter with ¼ cup melted chocolate chips. Top with cacao nibs and sliced strawberries or mangoes.

Directions

Cut the avocado in half lengthwise and twist to separate the halves. Remove the pit and scoop out the flesh using a spoon. Add the avocado and all remaining ingredients to a medium-size bowl. Using a hand mixer or food processor, blend until smooth and creamy. It may take a few minutes to get the avocado completely blended. Spoon the mousse into 4 small bowls and top each with one tablespoon of vanilla cashew cream.

You can enjoy this dessert right away, or better yet, let it firm up in the refrigerator for an hour or more.

Mini-Churro Twists

Makes about 18

Ingredients

1 tablespoon flax meal

3 tablespoons water

4 tablespoons nondairy butter

½ cup water

¼ cup unsweetened nondairy milk

1 teaspoon vanilla extract

¼ teaspoon salt

¾ cup flour

¼ cup sugar

¾ teaspoon cinnamon

Directions

Preheat oven to 400 degrees F and line a baking sheet with parchment paper. Mix the flax meal with water and set aside.

In a medium saucepan, add butter, water, milk and vanilla, and heat until the butter is melted and it all starts to bubble. Then add salt and flour and mix until a dough starts to form. Remove from heat, add in the flax egg and stir until just combined.

Let cool slightly and then portion out tablespoon-size pieces of dough onto your parchment-lined baking sheet, approximately 18 pieces. Next, take one piece of dough and break it in half. Roll each half between your hands, making two thin rods that are about 4 to 6 inches long and a little thicker than a pen. Take those two rods of dough and twist them together, forming a churro twist. Place the twist back on the baking sheet. Repeat with the rest of the dough.

Bake for 20 minutes or until just slightly golden on top. The churros should be crisp on the outside with the insides light and airy.

While the churros bake, mix the cinnamon and sugar in a medium-size bowl. Let the churros cool for 15 minutes once they're done baking. Then roll them carefully in the cinnamon sugar mixture. Eat these crispy treats on their own or dip them in rich chocolate sauce.

Chocolate Dipping Sauce

Ingredients

⅓ cup nondairy chocolate chips

¼ cup light coconut milk (from the can, not a carton)

In a small saucepan, add chocolate chips and coconut milk. Stir constantly over medium heat until smooth. Serve with the churros and watch everyone smile.

DESSERTS

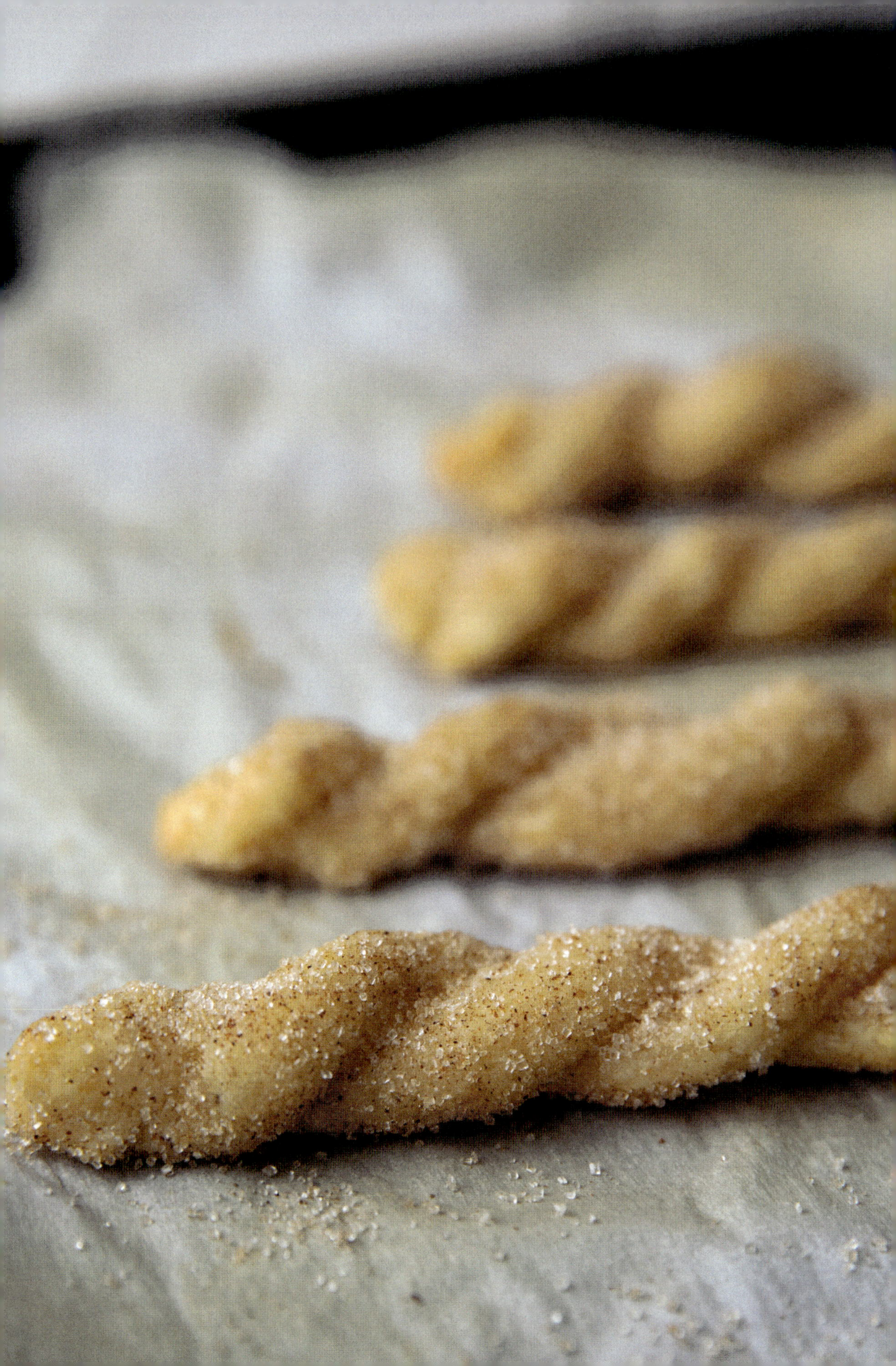

I met a pig named Jack

A few months before I began working for Best Friends in 2007, I was at Best Friends Animal Sanctuary for a visit and met a pig named Jack. It was my first real close-up experience with a pig of any kind and it smashed any preconceptions I had.

Jack could go for walks and he could follow cues like "sit." All the pot-bellied pigs at the Sanctuary's Marshall's Piggy Paradise had unique personalities. They were individuals. That realization broke down the walls I had put up in my mind about which animals were "worthy" of being saved and which animals were OK to eat. I knew I needed to stop believing that one animal's life carried less value than another, and I made the decision to become a vegetarian. And then, in time, I became a vegan. Today, I am proud to say that living my values has never been easier and tastier, and I know this cookbook will help you do the same, regardless of where you are on your journey.

Jon
Best Friends employee with Barney

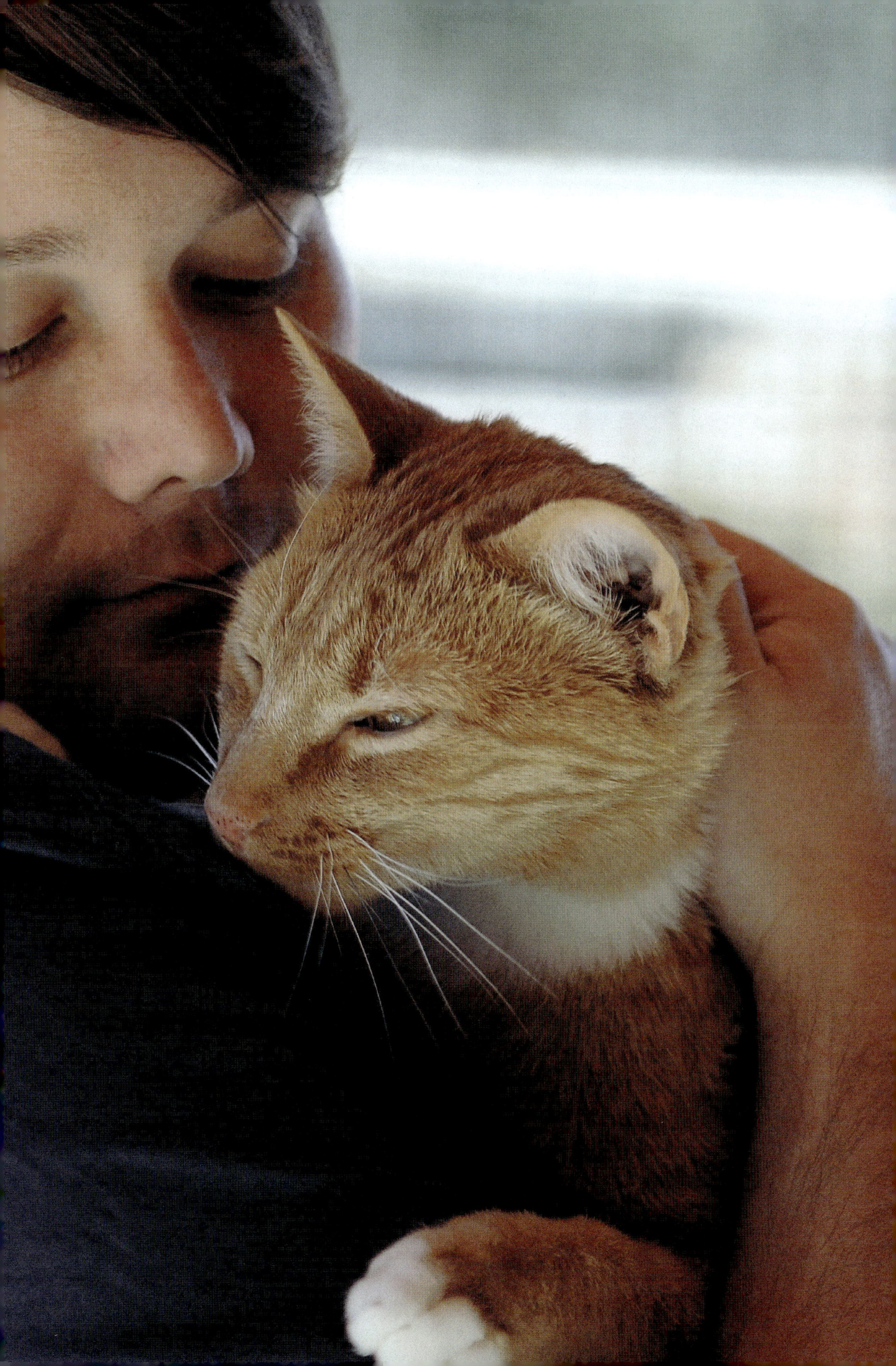

Recipes for Your Pet

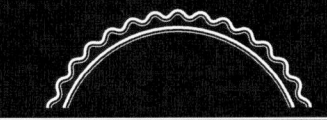

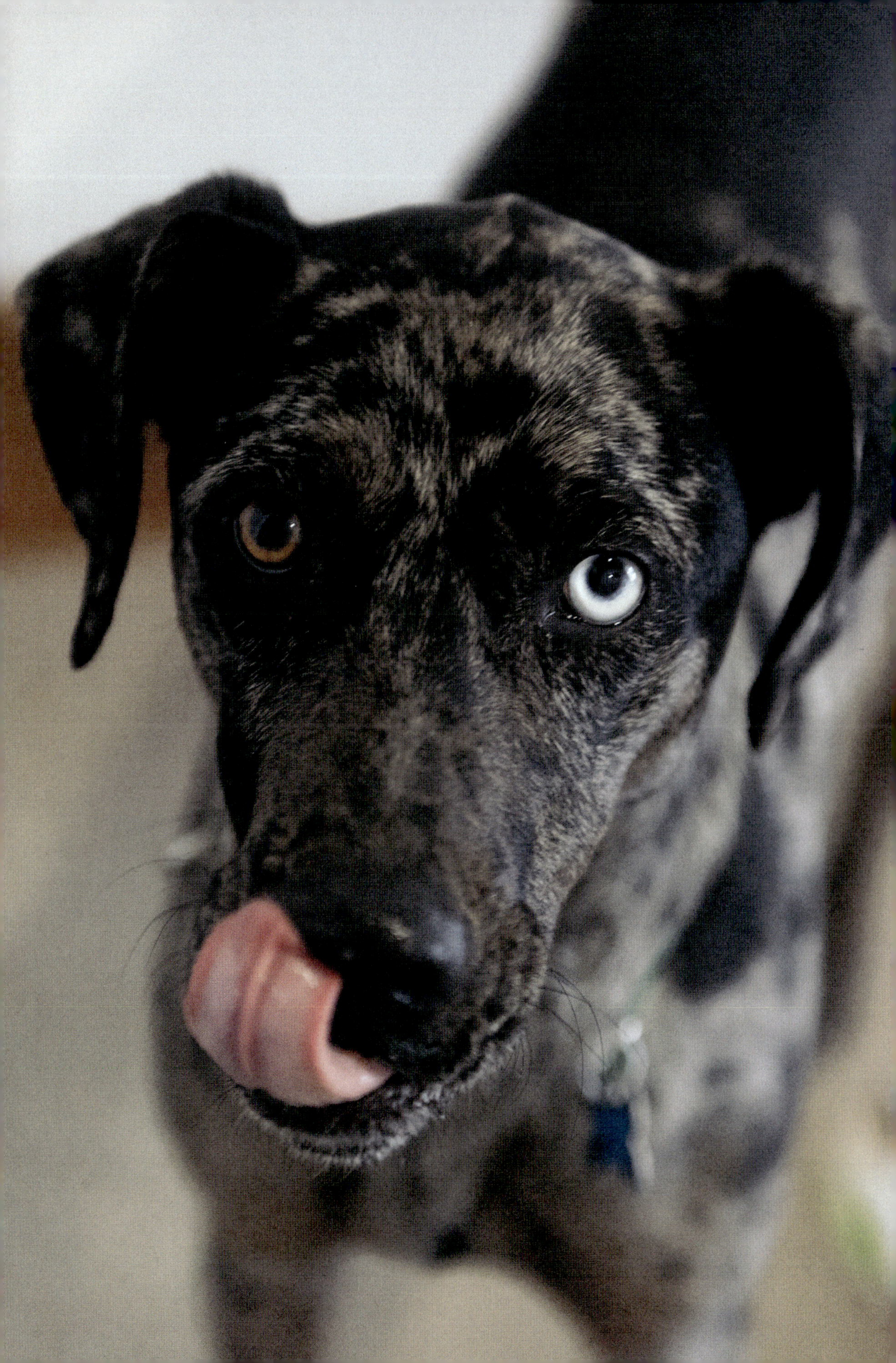

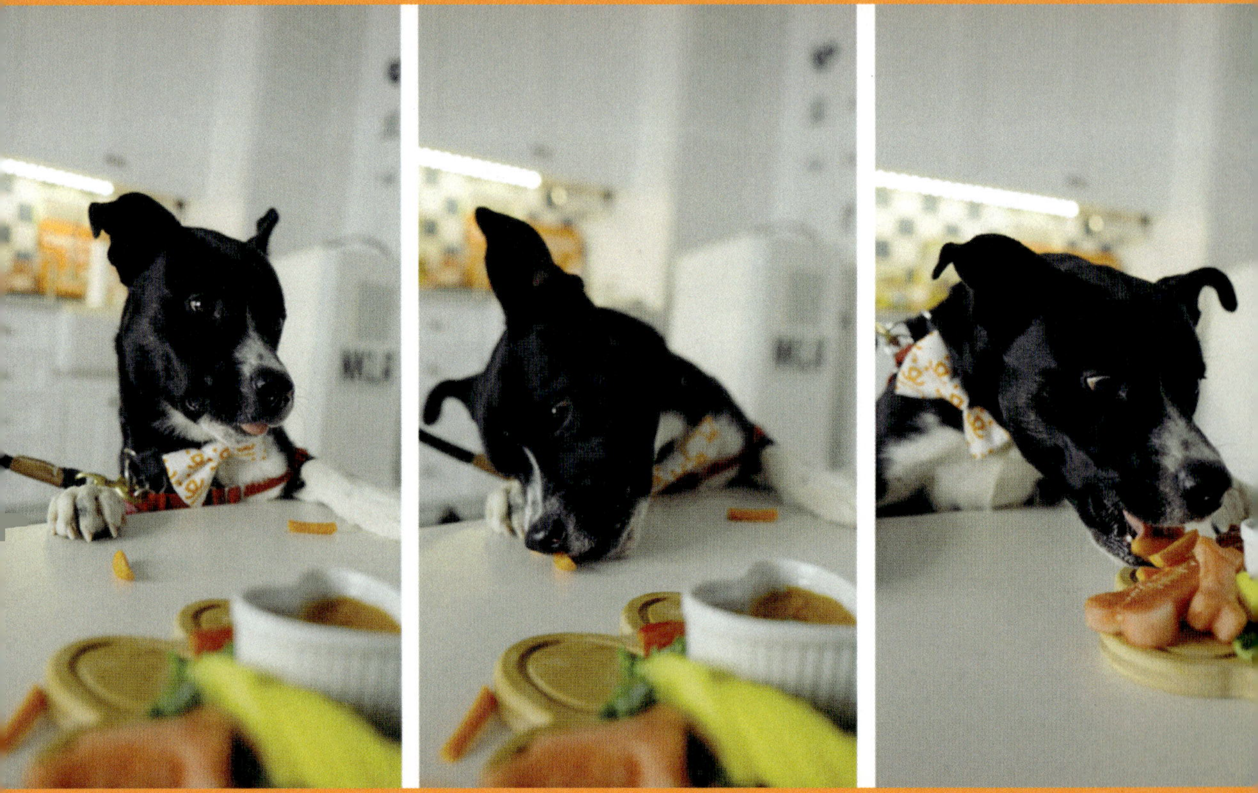

Barkcuterie Board

Best Friends in Los Angeles made "barkcuterie boards" for some lucky homeless pups. Here's how you can, too!

Ingredients

Dog-friendly fruits and vegetables*:

Pumpkin

Blueberries

Apple (no seeds)

Watermelon

Cucumbers

Broccoli

Kale

Carrots

Peanut butter (xylitol-free)

Kibble or canned food

Dog biscuits

Directions

Choose a board. Grab the treats of your choice.

Use cookie cutters for the dog-friendly fruit and veggies.

Spoon kibble or canned food into a ramekin.

Tuck a few treats under the kale or spinach.

Add a dab of peanut butter (xylitol-free) for special occasions.

Try this for any holiday or to give your dog a mouthwatering birthday surprise!

*Always check with your vet before introducing new foods your pet's diet.

Parrot Chop for Parrots

Ingredients

1 cup dry quinoa (about 3 cups cooked)

2 cups shredded purple cabbage

2 cups chopped snap peas

1 cup shredded carrot

1 cup diced red bell pepper

1 cup diced fresh mango

1½ cups beans of choice (such as edamame, black beans, or chickpeas)

½ cup nuts of choice (such as chopped peanuts, slivered almonds, or sunflower seeds for nut-free)

Directions

Cook the quinoa according to package instructions, then set aside to cool while you prepare everything else. Add all the veggies and beans to a bowl along with the cooked and cooled quinoa and combine. Mix everything together and top with nuts of your choice.

Parrot Pops

Ingredients

Gather your favorite parrot-safe fruits and vegetables:

Bananas	Broccoli
Grapes	Bell peppers
Oranges	Asparagus
Kiwis	Sweet potatoes

Directions

Chop the fruit and vegetables into small pieces. Fill ice cube trays with the chopped food. Pour water into the individual cubes to cover. Set a popsicle stick in each cube, then freeze the tray of treats and serve! The pops also work well without popsicle sticks.

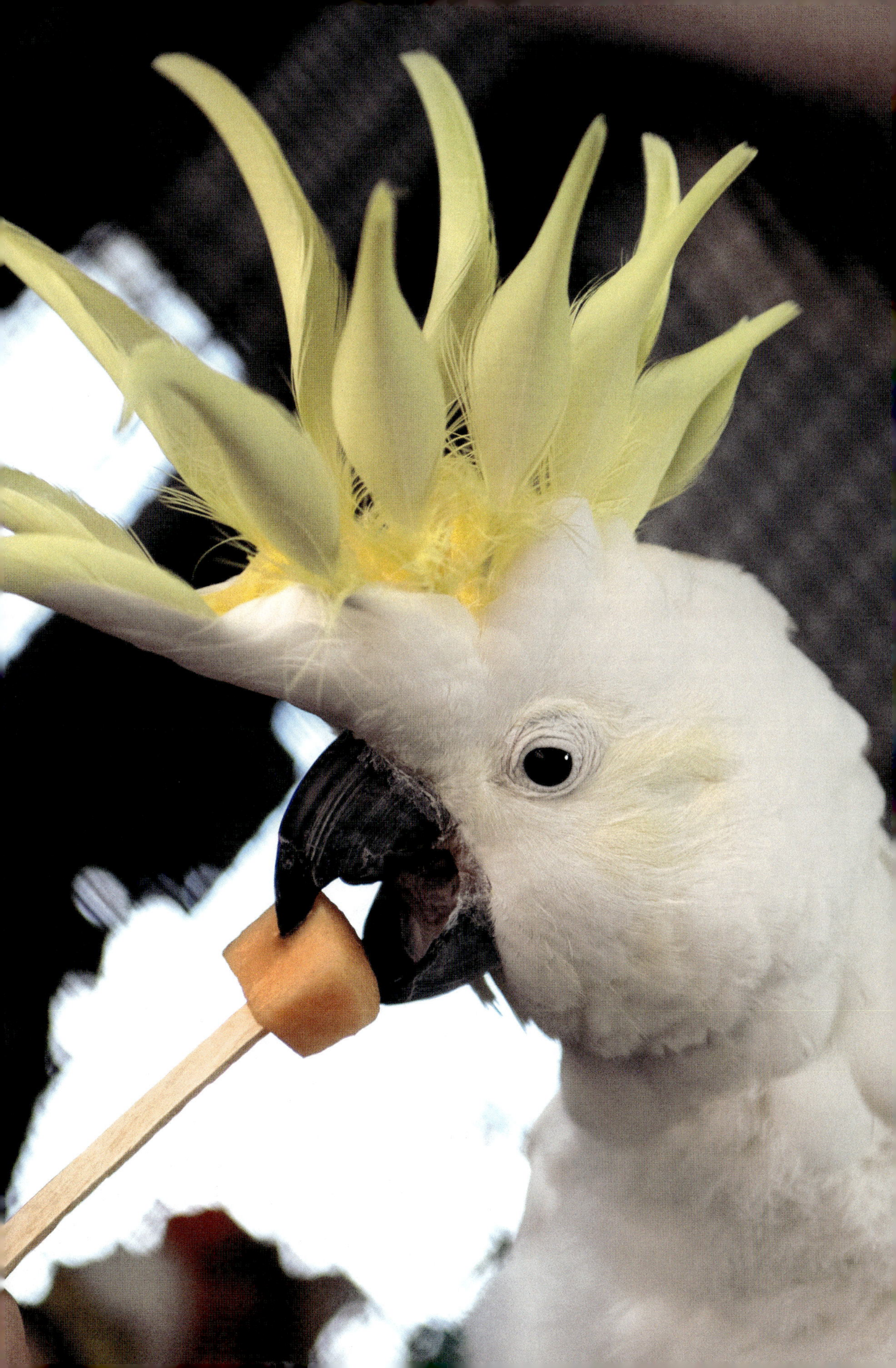

Kitty Upside-down Cake

Ingredients

One 5½-ounce can of kitty's favorite canned food. (Paté style works best.)

Crunchy treats (such as Greenies)

Decoration(s)

Squeezable cat treat, such as Churu or Applaws Puree

Catnip, fresh or dried (optional)

Oat grass (optional)

Directions

Open the cat food can and add a layer of crunchy treats on top. Lightly press the treats into the food so that they stick. Gently turn the can over and ease the food out onto the fanciest saucer your feline will eat from and voilà: kitty cake! (Alternatively, you can put a layer of treats on a saucer and carefully turn the can onto it.)

For extra feline fanciness, you can decorate with puree "icing." Just cut the corner off of the treat tube or pouch and get creative! Depending on the consistency of the puree, it may help to chill it first.

Add catnip "sprinkles" (dry or fresh) and sprigs of cat grass to look like candles.

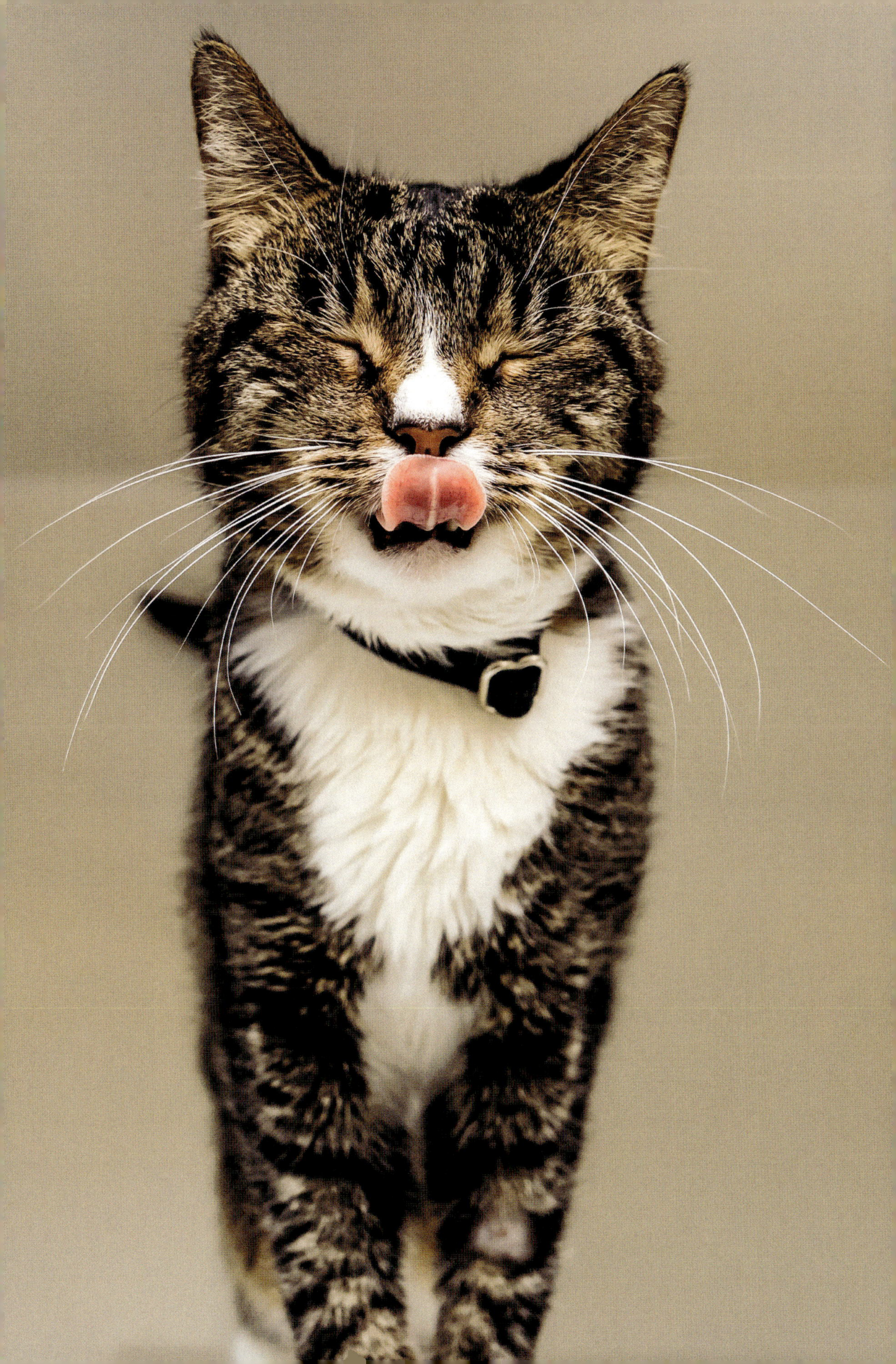

Best Friends Animal Sanctuary

There's no place like home.

When the founders of Best Friends came across Angel Canyon back in 1984, they knew it was a special place. In the gorgeous red rock country of southern Utah, they built an animal sanctuary like no other. Here, every life would be viewed as worth saving. Love, healing and second chances would be guaranteed for abandoned, neglected and abused pets. Best Friends Animal Sanctuary is a home-between-homes for up to 1,600 dogs, cats, bunnies, birds, horses, pigs and other barnyard animals. We hope you will come visit the Sanctuary to see this haven for yourself. And maybe you'll meet and adopt your new best friend.

While the Sanctuary will always be the heart and headquarters of Best Friends, Best Friends Animal Society's lifesaving work has spread far and wide. Best Friends has lifesaving programs from coast to coast, as well as lifesaving centers and teams in Los Angeles, Salt Lake City, New York City, Houston, Atlanta and Bentonville, Arkansas. We operate the Best Friends Network, which is made up of thousands of shelters, rescue groups and other animal welfare groups in all 50 states, working to save lives in their own communities. And we have programs nationwide that are helping to save the lives of community cats, end breed-specific legislation, shut down puppy mills and keep families and pets together.

Since we were founded, Best Friends has helped reduce the number of dogs and cats killed in shelters every year from an estimated 17 million to around 355,000. That's incredible progress but we won't stop until we Save Them All.

Each time you volunteer at a shelter, write a letter to your legislators, foster or adopt a pet, wear a Best Friends T-shirt or give this Best Friends cookbook to a friend, you help create a safer country and genuine kindness for all.

Everyone is welcome in the kindness kitchen. Let's all sit together at the same loving table!
Together, let's make history. Let's Save Them All.

Acknowledgments

As with all of Best Friends' work, this cookbook was a community project, a real collaboration of hearts and minds. We want to thank the following people for their talent, inspiration and contributions: Sarah Ause Kichas, Tracy Rizzi, BriAnne Figgins, Nichole Dandrea-Russert, M.S., RDN, Rebecca Cobb, Barbara Richardson, John Polis, Cyrus Mejia, Francis Battista and our recipe testers.

And a very special thanks to our crew at the Angel Village café.

Best Friends
Save Them All

Find out more about our lifesaving work and how you can be a part of it. Visit bestfriends.org.